THROUGH THEIR EYES

ANOTHER VIEW

Edited By Donna Samworth

First published in Great Britain in 2020 by:

Young Writers
Remus House
Coltsfoot Drive
Peterborough
PE2 9BF
Telephone: 01733 890066
Website: www.youngwriters.co.uk

All Rights Reserved
Book Design by Ashley Janson
© Copyright Contributors 2020
Softback ISBN 978-1-80015-081-2

Printed and bound in the UK by BookPrintingUK
Website: www.bookprintinguk.com
YB0451M

FOREWORD

Since 1991, here at Young Writers we have celebrated the awesome power of creative writing, especially in young adults, where it can serve as a vital method of expressing strong (and sometimes difficult) emotions, a conduit to develop empathy, and a safe, non-judgemental place to explore one's own place in the world. With every poem we see the effort and thought that each pupil published in this book has put into their work and by creating this anthology we hope to encourage them further with the ultimate goal of sparking a life-long love of writing.

Through Their Eyes challenged young writers to open their minds and pen bold, powerful poems from the points-of-view of any person or concept they could imagine – from celebrities and politicians to animals and inanimate objects, or even just to give us a glimpse of the world as they experience it. The result is this fierce collection of poetry that by turns questions injustice, imagines the innermost thoughts of influential figures or simply has fun.

The nature of the topic means that contentious or controversial figures may have been chosen as the narrators, and as such some poems may contain views or thoughts that, although may represent those of the person being written about, by no means reflect the opinions or feelings of either the author or us here at Young Writers.

We encourage young writers to express themselves and address subjects that matter to them, which sometimes means writing about sensitive or difficult topics. If you have been affected by any issues raised in this book, details on where to find help can be found at *www.youngwriters.co.uk/info/other/contact-lines*

CONTENTS

ACS Cobham International School, Cobham

Marion Sky Harper (13)	1

Admiral Lord Nelson School, Portsmouth

Riley Legg (12)	3
Harvey Bell (12)	4
George Croxford (12)	6
Molly Ellis (12)	8
Izzie Peachey (11)	10
Alex Marten (13)	12
Alyssa Pazvakavambwa (11)	14
Alex Pereira (13)	16
Yvie Bailey (12)	17
Tallulah Stanley (14)	18
Ryan Johnston (11)	19
Sophie Smith (11)	20
Lily Waites (14)	21
Olivia Underhill (12)	22
Saffrana Rahman (14)	23
Logan Smith (12)	24
Millie Warden (13)	25

Al-Islah Girls' High School, Blackburn

Ayesha Manzoor (14)	26
Khansa Zubair (14)	27
Aatika Mehmood (13)	28

All Saints Catholic Academy, Mansfield

Liana della-Spina (14)	29

Isabelle Beaver (12)	30
Hemn Warmington (12)	32
Faith Dion Williams (12)	34
Willow Hurst (12)	35
Niah Boyer-Blanchard (12)	36
Angel Stacey (12)	37
Chahat Marwaha (12)	38
Isabelle Chater (12)	39
Joshua Colclough (11)	40

Armadale Academy, Armadale

Abbie Sibbald (12)	41

Benfield School, Newcastle Upon Tyne

Harriet Pharoah (11)	42

Chace Community School, Enfield

Sherica Hlambelo (13)	43
Denzel Nwankwo (14)	44
Emily Pintacuda (13)	46
Abbie Holbrook (13)	48
Liam Viavattene (13)	50
Malgorzata Mikolajczak (18)	52
Cerys Dennett (12)	54
Anita (14)	56
Nehaan Mahamood (11)	57

De Stafford School, Caterham

Izzy Cronin (12)	58
Bethany Frost (12)	60
Emily Garratt (12)	62
Evie Lloyd (13)	64

Lily Edwards	66
Mallory Maguire (13)	68
Summer Cormack (12)	70
Harry Swanson (12)	71
Paige Bacon (14)	72
Joshua Walker (12)	74
Elliot McLaggan (11)	75
Markus Nilson (14)	76
Keya Khatri (13)	77
Tanner Bonds (14)	78
Rosie Gibbens (12)	79
Shane Cooper (13)	80
Hannah Crutchley (15)	81
Amy Nash (12)	82
Carys Byford (13)	83
Callum French (12)	84
Charlotte Groves (12)	85
Chloe E Smith (13)	86
Hollie Rubhunya (13)	87
Katie Bacon (14)	88
Ollie Moroney (15)	89
Zac Baker (11)	90
Ethan Sewell (13)	91

East Norfolk Sixth Form College, Gorleston

Lauren Wright	92
Ella Loades & Megan Hall	94

Farringdon Community Academy, Farringdon

Sam Elves (13)	95
Harrison Colley (12)	96
Victoria Rooks (15)	98
Chloe Hutchinson (12)	100
Jessica Hibberd (12)	101
Thomas Marshall (13)	102
Logan Tayim (12)	103
Bayleigh Maughan (11)	104
Ben Williams (11)	105
Ryan Soper (13)	106
Matthew Crabtree (14)	107

Ruby Large (12)	108
Heidi Smith (11)	109
Freya Nichol (12)	110
Deyanna Robinson (13)	111
Charlie Gettins (13)	112
Zac Schonewald (12)	113
Anna Gaffney (12)	114
Tamzin Facey (14)	115
Ben Howe (12)	116
Daynie Yeates (13)	117
Harley Waites (12)	118
Jacob Kay (12)	119
Josh Campbell (13)	120
Lili Farina (12)	121
Grace Terry (11)	122
Beki Wild (12)	123
Rhys Thompson (14)	124
Anton Haley (11)	125
Phoebe Croniin (11)	126
Maddison Marsh (11)	127
Ben Hanson (13)	128
Patrick Gokcan (11)	129
Ian Gage (12)	130
Sophie Chapman (11)	131
Darcie Taylor (13)	132
Kaitlyn McNeil (12)	133
Sophie Collins (11)	134
Dillan Howarth (11)	135

Kantor King Solomon High School, Barkingside

Khairun Nessa Momo (12)	136
Zak Cohen (11)	137
Rosie Preston (12)	138

St John's Marlborough, Marlborough

Niamh Taylor (13)	139
George Shepard (14)	140
Cerian Davies (12)	144
Emily Lappin (13)	146
Daisy Fry (13)	147
Lin Jun Zheng (12)	148

Sachen Heer	150
Oscar Holmes (12)	151
Evie Mundy (13)	152
Fonteyn Ip (14)	153
Guy Sainsbury (12)	154
Jia-Ling Yu (14)	155
Jacob Smith (13)	156
Madeline Wood (13)	157
Imogen Carter (12)	158
Alex Hawtin (14)	159
Sophie Elvey (12)	160
Thea Wratten (12)	161
Sian Hampshire (13)	162
Lucy Bartlett (13)	163
Ollie Watson (11)	164
Archie Balsdon (13)	165
Elsie Benneyworth (12)	166
Joe Bartlett (12)	167
Casey Berry (12)	168
Lauren Frost (13)	169
Nancy Nicholls (13)	170
Jontie Hart (11)	171
Elsie Monro (13)	172
Freddie Allen (13)	173
Tamzin Shipway (11)	174
Issy Nuttall (13)	175
Lewis Tearle (12)	176
Lucy Josey (13)	177
Isabel Barnett (12)	178
Beatrice Harvard Taylor (11)	179
Max Potter (13)	180
Alice Drowne (11)	181
Honey Lewis (12)	182
Thomas Norris (12)	183
Edie Liddiard (13)	184
Lucy Morris (13)	185
Stefan Pintilei (12)	186
Megan Greenhalgh (13)	187
Una Lenehan (12)	188
Lisa Nordlund (14)	189
William Mundy (11)	190
Oscar Atkinson (13)	191
Felix Sancto (12)	192
Theo Turner (12)	193
Lois Stevens (12)	194
Dakota Bessent (11)	195
Elina Pfeiler (13)	196
Alice Seddon (12)	197
Ted Rosedale (13)	198

The FitzWimarc School, Rayleigh

Zoe Webb (12)	199
Ben Harris (15)	200
Mia Warwick (12)	201
William Burling	202

THE POEMS

Lurking

Fangs, long as my forearm,
Eyes, red and cruel.
We all know why it lurks here,
It's hunting, now, for fuel.

I lie awake longing for sleep,
Not a clear sound to be heard.
My demons stay silent
As they slowly start to stir.

It's me they are hungry for,
While I wait all alone.
To them, human flesh is satisfying
To rip and tear from bone.

A howl shatters the silence.
I'm startled, waking, woken,
Just in time to see a maw
Gaping wide and open.

Rows and rows of sharp, sure fangs,
Teeth with blood on the tips.
Has it killed tonight already?
The beast snarls, and licks its lips.

It towers over me.
Its desire is clear.
To devour my body and soul
And feast upon my fear.

It looms ever closer,
A shadow coats my room.
The darkness creates a chance
For it to become a tomb.

I shriek, then it's over.
All is still, and then,
As morning comes and wakes me,
I wait for night to come again.

Marion Sky Harper (13)
ACS Cobham International School, Cobham

Extinction

My egg is cracking so I can have a little peep
And my sharp claws, through the egg it seeps
My feet pushing through, the bottom of the shell torn
And I burst out of my egg, to the world I am born
I have a look at some things, some big and some small
And a leaf-eating dinosaur, with a neck that's very tall
A dinosaur which looks like it has razor-sharp blades
And beaked things, with beaks, that look like the tips of blades.

Now I'm all big with razor teeth and not so whiny
But my hands are a bit weird because they are very tiny.
Brontosaurs and iguanodons I really like to gnaw
Their bones crunch into dust and their skin I just tore
Something scary and big from space comes and has struck
A big ball of rock, coming from the sky and in flames, I feel stuck.
It soon falls to the ground, causing a big boom,
And all my friends are sad because of impending doom.
Our world is in havoc, hell spreads everywhere
And you can see fire pretty much anywhere.
I soon die and am buried in a dirt coliseum
Where am I now? Well, in a history museum.

Riley Legg (12)
Admiral Lord Nelson School, Portsmouth

Warrior

One day, I was free and breathing, tall and cool,
The breeze brushed against my precious branches littered with leaves.
I was an emergent.
The bees pollinated on my thick branches,
Vines covered my stump.
I was an emergent.
Engines roared as my birds soared in the air,
My friends and neighbours fell around me
I looked down, all around was wood chips
I was an emergent.
Soon I fell down, I was chopped into small logs
And loaded into a truck
I was no longer an emergent.
I arrived at a factory that kills us trees and turns us into school books
I was picked up by a lift that took me to a conveyor belt
I was going to turn into paper!
I felt the saw cut me into small pieces
My precious wood as now paper.
I was put in a box van and loaded onto a huge ship
I rocked side to side,
Bashing against other boxes full of other pieces of paper just like me,
A blank page
I went to an English school called ALNS

I lived there for a few months,
Then I moved to a horrible black bin behind the school.
After the bin tipped over I flew to a huge body of water that disintegrated me. A fish ate me
(I was food!)
The fish was caught by a fishing net
Becoming a food that someone bought and ate.
Soon he died of food poisoning.

Harvey Bell (12)
Admiral Lord Nelson School, Portsmouth

The Robin Who Was Alone

Today is the day.
A day to be part of my flock, my friends, my people.
They all disagree with what I say but today will be different.
They'll have to trust me, they will have to trust me.
Planning this day has taken an eternity.
Thoughts after thoughts, days after days, I have seen it all.
Spiders, scorpions and snakes don't scare me anymore.
If this works, it will be the end.
After the attacks, our world has changed.
Nobody trusts anyone and all of us are endangered
They need my help and I won't let them stop me.
This cause is for the life of our kind.
I will not surrender my home and I will fight for what I believe in.
No matter what, no matter what!
I will become a hero, an icon, a god.
The time has come and war has begun.
I will not let them down.
I live alone and no one knows where.
The echoes of monkeys chanting and birds singing have stopped.
It has gone quiet ever since the attack.
It is ruined there, my home, is ruined.
There must be someone out there who can help our cause.
We are all dying, piece by piece, feather by feather!
My weapon might be enough - might - I do not know.

These creatures might be too powerful, however, I am their only hope.
I must keep fighting.

George Croxford (12)
Admiral Lord Nelson School, Portsmouth

Reality

The sky, bright and blue
The clouds, like a shelter
Trees...
The green leaves vibrant and solid
Spring is coming
Flowers blooming and the wind is calm
I stand here
What a view
The buzzing of bees
The flutter of wings
What a beautiful sight
The grass is fresh and green
Swaying in time with the gentle breeze
What's that noise I hear
Roaring up ahead?
Ouch, what's that I feel
Hitting hard all over me?
It's hail
Rain is coming down heavy
The grass is becoming wet
The wind is picking up speed
As I struggle to stand my ground
The flowers are hanging
And the trees are banging
Desperate for it to come to a halt
What a nightmare.

Am I hallucinating?
Is this all a dream?
Am I stupid enough to think it is real?
When will it stop...?
Will it stop?
The next day
Is a day of hell
A day of torture...
A trip to the seaside
Turning to a protest
Stop the plastic litter!
Stop it now!
The fish in the ocean
Innocent and harmless
All of a sudden
Can be drowned by food
Littering plastic can take an animal's life
One bit of plastic
That's all it takes...

Molly Ellis (12)
Admiral Lord Nelson School, Portsmouth

Help Me!

Help me
I have suffered pain
Pain I have never felt before
How do I tell? How do I say?
If I do what will happen?
Help me
I'm scared
Scared for my life
I hate school...
"Hey Fatty"
Please stop, please
Just keep quiet, it will be alright
Help me
I feel guilty
I can't tell anyone
I can hear the words in my head
"Fatty!" "Ugly!" "Tramp!"
Help me
I need to tell someone
This can't go on for any longer
"Mum, I need to tell you something"
"What? You're never like this..."
I open my mouth but the words are stuck
Come on, get out
I try but all that comes out is... "Don't worry"

Help me
I need to pluck up my courage
Please, please, please
I dread every moment of my life
I want to end it!
Help me
I need to tell someone but I can't
But I remember that I am worthy and that I can tell someone
"Um, Miss Jones, I'm being bullied. Help me please."
Happy me. Happy me
I have a big wide smile across my face
I don't have to see those boys anymore
So I can just be *me.*

Izzie Peachey (11)
Admiral Lord Nelson School, Portsmouth

Phone Poem

As soon as the password gets entered
I see the bad.
Instagram is flashing
@gamer11112 wants to follow you
@anieg112 posted for the first time
Stop! Stop! Stop!
I get flashes every four minutes
Just one more game
And I'll overheat
In a minute I'll be in the trash can
Just like my mate, he is there now
Nothing
Argh! Help!
I'm 2%
I'm nearly dead!
Please give me some juice
Or I'll be no use!
At the repair shop
The men tear me apart
Prodded and poked with the sharp screw head
My screen comes off
And I feel I am lost
Please, I beg, *get a decent case*
I feel all fresh, lovely and clean
It almost feels like I have had a shower
But then I think, *I won't have any power!*

They will probably buy an expensive friend of mine
'Cause I'm too old
I'm no use to people like them
Apparently, I go too slow
Maybe because you drop me too much!
Not again
They've just dropped me down the drain
All that cash
And I'm now trash
I'm just so harassed!
Dead!

Alex Marten (13)
Admiral Lord Nelson School, Portsmouth

Dear Earth

We are killing the Earth and that's really 'fun'
Adults don't believe us because we are young
Our forests are turning into ash in a second
Ask Australia, they will tell you about it
They'll tell you how they have lost all their homes
While Trump posts online and tweets on his phone
'Global warming is inexpensible to hoax!'
I'm gonna say this again,
This is *not* a joke!
Factories are working
And toxins are
As we're trying to breathe
Our future is stolen and we are the thieves
The sea levels are rising
The ice caps are melting
The corals are crying
And no one is helping!
Do you know they all keep the ocean alive!
This started back in the 1980s!
Don't come to me when your child can't think
Of what a tiger is because they're extinct
Don't cry to me when your faux coat ain't clean
The endangered list is now 41,416...
Dear our precious Earth,
Do you think we're gonna survive...?

If you end up reading this poem, I just wanna say...
I'm sorry.

Alyssa Pazvakavambwa (11)
Admiral Lord Nelson School, Portsmouth

A Star Is Born

I had a wish...
but not just a wish.
It was a wish, of having a sister!
And then one lovely and quiet night,
I looked up the sky
and the loveliest and cutest star appeared
between all the others that were scattered everywhere
across the night sky.
My wish had come true!
It was like someone was offering me a present...
but... a special one.
It was all I could imagine and hope for,
and now I had it!
My heart started to warm up like I was in a hot tub.
Suddenly I opened my eyes and realised it was all just a dream!
Tears started to rapidly fall out of my eyes
but then my parents appeared with a baby in their arms...
Was this the reality?

Alex Pereira (13)
Admiral Lord Nelson School, Portsmouth

Social Media

You get home from school
You think you are so cool
But little do you know
There is a word you don't know
The word is spreading like a cough
Or a bomb going off
You should know what it is called
You turned it into a ball
The word is bullying
You bullied a lot
Now it's your turn to be caught
You might be taken down to the basement
It's all your fault
It started as a joke
Not all the fake hate
You are now the bait
You should have run away
It should have been the day
You started this madness
Now you are just a mess
And you cannot get away
Now your phone is barking at you
You just have to hide away.

Yvie Bailey (12)
Admiral Lord Nelson School, Portsmouth

Why Me?

I see my home turning to dust,
These heartless humans destroyed our nature,
Our eyesight becomes weak,
Our skin has burned,
Only a couple of humans are trying to save our world,
The smoke steams up my eyes and gets into my lungs,
Why would these humans destroy our fun?
I'm all alone,
Scared... worried,
What will happen next?
When will the world know it's enough?
I sit in my tree, my body filled with grief,
The fires are expanding,
More dirty, dangerous chemicals are getting thrown into my home,
The air chokes me but yet I've got to breathe,
Mother Nature, if you are there
We need help...

Tallulah Stanley (14)
Admiral Lord Nelson School, Portsmouth

Dusk And Dawn

Days and nights go past as quickly as they start.
The dusk and dawn are the most active
as if by silence they fly,
owls fly by dusk then dawn
every dusk
and every dawn of their life
with their family counting on them
but they sometimes don't come back.
What if I told you that we are the cause?
We kill them without knowing
we put poison on our plants to stop the mice and rats
but we are killing owls
we just don't know how wonderful owls are
but if we don't stop they will be gone
and it will be our fault.

Ryan Johnston (11)
Admiral Lord Nelson School, Portsmouth

My Cat, Buzz

His name is Buzz,
He does, yes, love,
He will cuddle you,
Even if you're new,
He loves sponge cake,
And he loves to give us presents like mice,
Just as we awake,
He can sit on command, so there's no need to worry,
And do not feed him a McFlurry,
He loves his food,
And if you're wondering he is not rude,
His fur is black and he has a white chin,
Which might make you feel like you want to get a gin,
He loves it when you scratch behind his ears,
We love him lots and we've had him for three years.

Sophie Smith (11)
Admiral Lord Nelson School, Portsmouth

Pandora

The anger I feel
Can break a mother's aching heart.
I fear I can never heal,
As my family and I part.
The cursed box;
Has ruined many lives.
Never escaping the rusted locks,
That destroy innocent hearts with actions like knives.
Those scarred souls as they suffer in silence;
Fading away into a fearful and forgotten past
As we form a deadly alliance.
This world of woeful suffering: endless. Vast.
If only it wasn't for that wretched witch
Who left a chasm in the world no god can stitch.

Lily Waites (14)
Admiral Lord Nelson School, Portsmouth

The Black Horse

Blackened hooves, a matching mane.
Through the fields she will reign.
Over the pasture's floor of green.
Look closely. Only then she will be seen.
A warm and quiet night in June.
Eyes that twinkle under the full moon.
The young filly will dash at the stroke of midnight.
Rearing, bucking, running, slipping and sliding just out of spite.
Soon the night will end.
The filly will retire upon the ground.
But the sun will rise once again.
And the little black filly,
Will have a new day to begin.

Olivia Underhill (12)
Admiral Lord Nelson School, Portsmouth

Here We Go Again

Here we go again...
The butterflies in my tummy
The chats, the snaps
Disagreements with strangers
Not knowing the dangers
Depression and anxiety
Just words with no meaning
Just words floating in space
Taking selfies and photos for the world to see
Opening your eyes to non-existent insecurities
Why do we do this?
Torture our mind, overthink and over examine
Another day, another like
Here we go again...

Saffrana Rahman (14)
Admiral Lord Nelson School, Portsmouth

Pigeon

Pigeon be going zoom
Zooming through the skies
And squawking a lot
Men and women throw objects
Putting pigeon off track
He crashes and there is a mighty loud smack
But he gets up again
His back is hurting
When he gets up in the sky
He finds out his wings have to dry
When he gets down
The floor is wet and the grass is soft
His wing soon dries off
And he goes to the tree
And meets with his family.

Logan Smith (12)
Admiral Lord Nelson School, Portsmouth

The Rescue

Will my dream ever come true?
As I slept on the thought of a new life
My heart cried longingly for a family of my own.
I woke up feeling unwanted
Until a family peered into my cage at my sad, tired eyes
Next thing I knew I was put in the back of the car,
Children stroking my soft, furry coat
Was this my fresh new start?
When we pulled up outside the house,
My heart raced
I panted in excitement.

Millie Warden (13)
Admiral Lord Nelson School, Portsmouth

Games

Black skies, my hands are cold,
Fallen angels that don't fit the mould,
Hollowed out hearts that I now hold,
Locked up with chains, but I can't be controlled.

Deadly silence that can't be heard,
Broken wings on broken birds,
I look at you, your face is blurred,
No need to say a single word.

Frozen fire, that's way too hot,
Pull the trigger, he's heard the shot,
Staring you down, standing silently on the spot,
Now that I have got your attention, it's time for the final plot.

Your words are bullets, your mouth's a gun,
Let's change it up, this game is no fun,
You should have known, this won't help you in the long run,
No turning back now, the games have already begun.

Ayesha Manzoor (14)
Al-Islah Girls' High School, Blackburn

Fifteen Seconds Of Fame

The camera switches on,
and the smile appears,
but in reality it's just a con.
I take a break, wipe the tears,
no one knows about the fears.

Behind the screens that they hold,
I'm not really that bold.
I wish It wasn't fake,
but now I cry a lake.

I try to be happy,
but their comments are just so snappy.
I wish I could block out all the noises
but loud are the voices.

They all think I'm happy,
but their words make me feel crappy.
The more fame I gain,
the more I feel pain.
They don't know their words hurt,
but they put me in the dirt.
From here on I won't be there
even if they do care.

Khansa Zubair (14)
Al-Islah Girls' High School, Blackburn

The Sea Of Life

Life is like an endless sea,
You never know where it's going to end.
You never know when the storm will hit,
Crashing down on you, destroying your every hope.
Wondering why you were the victim,
When there were so many more to choose from.
You never know when the sun will be taken away,
Replaced by black skies.
You never know when the boat will sink,
When you are enveloped by the evil sea of life.

Aatika Mehmood (13)
Al-Islah Girls' High School, Blackburn

Discriminate Me

Like a small child full of love and emotions
Standing out from the world in its different oceans.
How this tiny hope can make any heart open
They may only have one chance to make this explosion.

There was so much more they could have said
Like heavyweights inside their head.
Screaming out to the world in the bright night
When can you not hear their voice in this dark light?

Hear their song of this fight they will win
Taking back their nights from those that sin.
Proving their power and to show they are strong
We celebrate those who fight with their song.

Now the battle is nearly at its end
And this poor child is in need of a friend
From what disease of colour came
You must entrust people to fight their own game.

Even if no one else will ever believe
I still have got a fight which is left in me.

Liana della-Spina (14)
All Saints Catholic Academy, Mansfield

Sides

There are two different sides to everyone.
But you probably can't see,
Two different sides to everyone,
That means even you and me.
If you want to witness the two sides you'll need to find the key,
That unlocks the divergent parts of the human anatomy.

While one side can be dark,
The other can be bright.
One side can leave a mark
While the other gives out light.

One side can flee
While the other will protect
One part will give
But the other will just reject.

One of the sides is joyous
While the other side is just upset.
One side will have found true love
The other will only just have met.

There are two sides to everyone
But you probably can't see.
Two different sides to everyone
That means even you and me.

If you want to witness the two sides you'll just need to find the key
That unlocks the divergent parts of the human anatomy.

Isabelle Beaver (12)
All Saints Catholic Academy, Mansfield

With War Comes Sacrifice

I fly high in the sky,
In a land that I used to own.
I watch the soldiers pass by,
Everyone seems to be alone.

I fight on the side of light,
Of freedom, rights and will.
For my wings take flight
Because I see the witch stands still.

Flames fly from my breath,
I thought we had the upper hand.
But it hurts the witch no less,
Then I can't lift off the ground.

I am on the ground,
I can't move my tail.
The witch curses my body all around,
For stone grows up my skin, there is no tale.

Thoughts rush through my head,
Did I choose the right side?
There is no hope now for my eyes go red,
So now this is my fate I have to abide.

One hundred years go by,
I can still remember being in the sky.
But still I sit,
For the curse still holds me in this pit.

But I remember the wise words,
With war comes sacrifice.

Hemn Warmington (12)
All Saints Catholic Academy, Mansfield

The Roles Reverse

I feel the warm grasp of a hand,
Let's just hope I'm not lost in the sand.
The cold hand throws me in a pocket,
It's time to escape, I must leave like a rocket!

Footsteps are louder now,
I jump and bounce, making a loud sound.
Light comes back to me, it's time to leave this town,
Everything at once, those humans make us bow.

Now I am free I cannot give up,
Not right now, I haven't had enough.
If I can reach it in time,
My problems will be solved without a crime.

I made it through, look at me go,
Us objects aren't that slow.
This is where my chapter ends,
Unlike most keys, I'm not the one who defends.

Faith Dion Williams (12)
All Saints Catholic Academy, Mansfield

The Pen

I've travelled far and wide,
To where I have laughed and cried,
I've searched this Earth,
Looking for ways to prove my worth.

I've been in many hands,
As many as grains of sand,
Both good and bad,
Both happy and sad,
I've been in many hands.

Shakespeare, Dickens, Dahl,
Crippen, Hitler, Khan,
So many people, so many friends,
To whom my help I did lend.

I've been in many hands,
As many as grains of sand,
Both good and bad,
Both happy and sad,
I've been in many hands.

I gave my all,
But I was doomed to fall.
Cast aside due to age,
Time to turn a new page.

Willow Hurst (12)
All Saints Catholic Academy, Mansfield

Life As A Ballet Shoe

I've been around the world
I've seen theatres big and small
I've made dreams come true for generations
But now
I'm none of that at all.
I've felt the pain
I've seen the tears
I've been separated
Reunited
But now
I'm forgotten.
Just an old heirloom
I hear them say
"Nothing special."
This isn't the life I want to lead
I need someone to revive me
Then I hear footsteps
And a giggle
I will fulfil another dream
My life as a ballet shoe will start again.

Niah Boyer-Blanchard (12)
All Saints Catholic Academy, Mansfield

Dolly

The amazing doll
All beautiful and sweet
Two long pigtails
Hang by her eyes
And always is a baby
Through little children's eyes.

But they start to grow
Up they will truly see
"This is too small for me!"
So she has gone
She has been shipped away
She is now on the streets
And there the dolly lays.

Until a girl comes along
All lovely and jolly
Now all over again
She is the girl's dolly.

Angel Stacey (12)
All Saints Catholic Academy, Mansfield

Life As A Camera

The life of a camera,
A beautiful life it is.
I have always been part of a family,
Never left out.

I have seen spectacular places,
From Mexico to America to Italy.
So many memories,
So many happy, excited faces.

People telling me how they feel,
Telling me their pain and joy.
I have kept every memory safe,
Safe like a loving family member.

The life of a camera,
A beautiful life it is.

Chahat Marwaha (12)
All Saints Catholic Academy, Mansfield

The Gleaming Warmth

The glistening green
The gleaming warmth
My hopes, my dreams
Locked away for all inside
Beady eyes shoot back at me
A small reflection angry as can be
So I run, I run, I run
For one final push
Away with it I run
To keep for me and my family
Joyful as can be
She places it back so gently
As she walks away
She begins to whisper
I love you.

Isabelle Chater (12)
All Saints Catholic Academy, Mansfield

The Life Of A Money Box

Discovered
Disposed of onto the streets
Picked up by a man
Journey
Placed in a bag
Thrown into a car
Fullness
Man places metallic circular objects into me
Warmth from coins
Emptiness
As man takes coins
Cold darkness inside.

Joshua Colclough (11)
All Saints Catholic Academy, Mansfield

Through Their Eyes

I love you, big sister, with all of my heart,
I think you're so funny, amazing and smart.
You are what I want to be when I am older,
You show me how to be brave and bolder.

I listen and watch you every time you are near,
I always feel so safe when you are here.
You often encourage me to do my best,
You help support me to figure out the rest!

But sometimes you don't seem to want me around,
You want your peace, you tell me not to make a sound.
It hurts my feelings because you just don't know,
How much I need you to help me grow.

I know that I'm younger and like different things,
But when you play with me it makes my heart sing!
I love being around you whenever I can,
From your little sister - your biggest fan!

Abbie Sibbald (12)
Armadale Academy, Armadale

The Guard

The choking smoke that rules the sky,
Hear the trains scream, make children cry,
Watch the guard cut our hair,
Families dying everywhere.

Bliss and happiness is not a part of our mind,
For all our dreams have been left behind,
You can see the ghosts in our eyes,
All of our family that has died.

Hear the train's clickety-clack,
That very sound takes me back,
The train that took us to our doom,
Where we were trapped in one room.

Working too hard every day,
Praying that we would be saved one day,
We worked until our backs would break
What hurt the most was how our hearts ached.

Run, run, run as fast as you can,
You can't catch us but the Nazis can,
Of all the memories I could have spared,
I still see... the guard's glare.

Harriet Pharoah (11)
Benfield School, Newcastle Upon Tyne

What They See

Waking up each morning
Not knowing what the day will bring
Facing a world that doesn't know how to face you back

Tell me why each day
I have to fear for my life?
I might get shot down by a cop
Or stabbed with a knife

I could get beaten down
Or much worse
For not even reaching for a gun
But trying to get my purse

Seeing brothers and sisters getting killed
By the people we are supposed to trust
They receive no punishment for it
This is just so unjust

They roam the streets freely
Like they didn't commit murder
Acting like they are an innocent person
When the consequences should go much further

Through their eyes
They see a thug
But through my eyes
I see someone who just needs a hug.

Sherica Hlambelo (13)
Chace Community School, Enfield

The School Poem

When I finished Year 6 I was moving to a new school.
I met Chace Community in Year 7 and it was crucial.

People bully me because of my special needs,
They couldn't care about my life and my other deeds.

Beyond the thoughts my life is defined,
I'm thinking a secondary state of mind.

When I was younger, I used to love drawing back then,
But nowadays it gets tougher and again.

Something so hard goes straight to the soul;
It seems impossible to get over and my heart is left with a big hole.

I'm trying to be happy, wearing a smile; but I'm dying inside.
The world seems to be fading, and I just want to run and hide.

When I first met Year 10, it was too painful,
But then, I was fighting for freedom and for this school.

When school ended, I felt lonely,
I went home and I asked God to keep me holy.

When I was in Year 9, I was doing my final exams,
I was too worried that I couldn't pass the programs.

When life is sad, pools of darkness sweep through the school,
To prove that life is cruel.

My thoughts and others were blind,
I'm thinking a secondary state of mind.

When I look in the mirror, I only see darkness,
I will change life and sort the hardness.

When I'm so sad, I am so defined
I'm thinking a secondary state of mind.

It seems like just a blink ago I first held myself in one arm,
It's been my job to love, to teach, to keep me safe from harm.

So when I wave goodbye in a moment, I will turn to walk inside
Forgive me if I crumple into tears of loss and pride.

This poem is for my grandma's mum that passed away,
In loving memory we pray.

Denzel Nwankwo (14)
Chace Community School, Enfield

Web Of Lies

Only a few words were said,
But they were wrapped around her finger,
She was the monster under my bed,
And my friends were like sheep whilst they linger.
The person I thought I could trust betrayed me,
I was wronged by the people I tried to protect,
They started to act coldly towards me,
And her *lies* were left unchecked.

She wanted to keep them in a cage of *lies*,
I tried setting them free,
Yet all they did was criticise,
My pathetic attempts stopped when I realised,
They don't think about me.
I could point out all that was wrong.
But if they were true…
If our friendship was strong…
Would I really have to?

Was my use simply to provide?
And have nothing in return?
Are my feelings to be put aside?
Despite all I've done, their backs are turned…
If she would win…
Then the prize is not worth my time.
My fight for them was in vain
I was just a tool for their blame

I guess her torture helped me in some way,
They all said: I am your friend,
But today was the day,
I found out, that it was just pretend.
Now they've shown their true colour.
My friendship with them has come to an end.
The adults won't excuse her behaviour
Instead they left me to fend.

They thought I was a traitor.
But now it is time to show them,
That my friendship cannot be used for free labour,
That despite being condemned
I will survive,
They will try to break me.
But my soul won't feed on her web of *lies*,
In the end I will be free.

Emily Pintacuda (13)
Chace Community School, Enfield

Mind

My mind begins to wander and my heart begins to pound,
No messages to read, no calls and no one is around,
The darkness creeps into my soul and the world begins
to whirl
The pain is real, the fear is crippling, my fingers start to curl,
I am stuck inside my shrinking shell, it's easy to disappear
No one sees the real me because the smiles can hide
the fear.
This illness is not rational, it's hard to understand
How a person who seems to have everything can still feel
so bad
To hide away but long to be seen, to know that people care
To hold you close, to not let go, to show you they are there
One day I will feel better but today is a struggle
It's amazing the effects on someone with just a
single cuddle
The darkness they feel overshadows the light
No matter how much they try they are losing the fight
But don't give up on them, two are stronger than one
Show that together any battle can be won.
Start off with the small things, take a little at a time
Show them that together even the errors are just fine
Let them cry if they need too and shout if they must
But show them that with you they have unconditional love
and trust.

Please don't give up when they are down but show them that you are always around
It's amazing how much better they will feel when their true self is found.

Abbie Holbrook (13)
Chace Community School, Enfield

One Chromosome Ahead

Every day life is not the same,
You are always worrying and thinking instead,
It's hard to answer so you get the blame,
For everyone who is one chromosome ahead.

Special schools and special treatment.
Living is so much harder as you grow,
But someone like this you should know,
Shouldn't have to feel so different.

My brother is one I look up to,
He finds it hard but he may not show it,
But he carries on, even when he is blue,
And although he struggles, he shows great spirit.

It must be hard to live in a world,
Where you're second picked in all you do,
But in your conformist society, you should be told,
Of nice and kind people there are few.

This is a message that should be expressed more,
Whether here, there, everywhere and furthermore,
Spread the word rather than being misled,
That a person is no different if they are one chromosome ahead.

Now if you are one of those who discriminate,
Who has not yet realised what has just been said,

It is not too late to change your mind's state,
And think of the people who are one chromosome ahead.

Liam Viavattene (13)
Chace Community School, Enfield

I Am

When you are eighteen you should be an adult,
your feelings and emotions in check,
plans made, path picked
ready to set off, but

I'm not saying I'm not
prepared. Just some time
some things change,
feelings, sentiments, memoirs,

like roses in summer, bloom
and their petals fall, like
tears from eyes, preparing
the red carpet that will cover

our path, when you're eighteen
you feel embarrassed to ask
your mum for a hug, just a
hug, who else feels like that?

Put your hand up! Please.
Tell me that hand which
grasps my throat so strong
is not imaginary. That this flood

of love and hatred, this social cage,
others feel too, I am eighteen and
I am myself, self-made, self-expressed,
shaped. I want to try

to sail down the river and
explore the wide, wild world.
Do things my way! Fall, fail, rise,
triumph.

But the rider of the tombs, the inventor of the new.
the explorer of the strange, brave heart within,
like a lion that says, "That's my territory!"
I'm eighteen and I have bloomed.

Malgorzata Mikolajczak (18)
Chace Community School, Enfield

Earth

Dear Future Existence,
It's Earth here
Global warming, forest fires, plastic in my oceans, animals dying
It's all down to you
What crazy, destructive stunt are you going to pull next?
When I am suffering, burning and dying no one helps me
People use their phones to say *#savetheplanet*
But they are not saving me because they are giving out their carbon footprint
Killing me one step faster
People like you leave lights on even when you are not in the same room
Why do you do that?
You don't think about the damage you are causing?
Even when I am the reason you are alive
I am the place that you call home, but that won't be the case for much longer
Since I am the one you are destroying
While you are living your life my life is becoming extinct
Burnt to ash
Why can't it be how it used to be when I was young?
Ice was everywhere you looked
I felt cool
Now everywhere I look I see screens and skyscrapers

All I feel is a thick blanket of fire
If you have found this letter I am sorry
Yours sincerely
Earth.

Cerys Dennett (12)
Chace Community School, Enfield

Gods

They sit up high on golden thrones,
Silver running along ivory bones,
They're puppeteers playing with their toys,
Laughing in their minds, creating such noise,
Oh ignorant humans, bliss coating their mind,
Complacent with the control, because it feels so kind,
But gods stay laughing as they cut the string,
Now they only have the darkness to cling,
Whispers creep round corners, you're helpless you're ours,
So humans push out the words, heads at ease,
While every so often they see the shadows and freeze.

For gods it's such a delight,
When even the day turns to dark night,
And their power grows, as each little prayer is heard,
Each undeserving word.

Anita (14)
Chace Community School, Enfield

Never Judge

New year, new you
New school, new books, new teachers
It's a new age and a new decade
New month, new news,
New resolutions, new hobbies
Guess what?
New year, new you.

Nehaan Mahamood (11)
Chace Community School, Enfield

The Small Bed In The Large Hospital

I thought I knew where to go,
But turns out that isn't true.
All I need to do is get away from the small bed in the large hospital,
It's stealing the reality of life away from me,
I demand to see my family.
Before the two decades of my life is turned to ash.

The wind is bitter as I leave the building behind,
My head is starting to thump,
But I am going to keep on moving.
All I need to do is get away from the small bed in that large hospital.

The sun is setting,
Temperature's dropping,
The cold surrounds me and consumes me.
All I need to do is get away from the small bed in that large hospital.

I wish I had one place to rest until dawn,
But no one is willing to share a room with me.
A hideous, towering, slender eyesore like me.
All I need to do is get away from the small bed in that large hospital.

I have spotted my enemies sprinting down pathways,
Pointing their fingers,
Shouting, "That's him!"
They are all dressed identically,
Clinical blue robes that reach past their knees,
And a mask covering mouth and nose.
They are going to hunt me, I am their prey,
They are the wolves,
I can't give up, although it doesn't look like I have a choice... but still,
All I would like to do is get away from the small bed in the large hospital.

Izzy Cronin (12)
De Stafford School, Caterham

Alzheimer's

People are shouting at me from left, right and centre.
Do you know what it is like to have people shouting at you, saying, "Do you remember?"
I have Alzheimer's, I am not deaf.
'Do you remember me?' is a very stupid question to ask someone like me.
I am not scared to hide it.
But I'm not exactly proud of it.

Imagine not being able to live in your home, the one you have lived in all your life.
To be a danger to yourself.
Well, that is me, and I am it.
You have no idea how my life has changed these past few years.

The feeling of hope that you just may be allowed to go home.
Waiting for the nurse to come in and give you the news.
Wondering whether there's any point in holding on to the one shred of hope, of independence and dignity.
Everything's falling apart.
I have no control over it.

She's walking towards me, I can't tell whether it's good or bad news.
He face is expressionless.
I'm shaking with nerves as thoughts go through my head:
Will I ever see home again?

The nurse is just about to get a doctor.
Strangers are with me to hear the news but I don't want them to hear.
I don't know them.

Bethany Frost (12)
De Stafford School, Caterham

A Little Look Closer

At first glance, I'm your average teen.
Short hair, backpack.
But there's something different, something strange.
Look a little closer and take a good look
Because there is much more to cover,
So, so much more,
Just look a little closer and look inside,
Look at my wellbeing and my mind.
My mind is a dark place.
At first glance, it's a weird and wonderful place,
But dig deeper, look closer.
In-between all that there are shadows,
Unnaturally long shadows.
They wriggle and writhe, slowly engulfing everything they find.
Slowly taking over, taking control.
But what's controlling them?
What's their help?
Take a step back.
Look around,
Look at the others as they scream and shout.
Why are they pointing at me?
What's it about?
Well, this is what casts these shadows.
What they say does not show
But it still casts shadows.

So when you see that lonely girl in the corner
Or that strange boy that has no friends
Look a little closer,
Open the book,
Walk forwards and have a closer look
Because in these eyes are shadows
Long and strong
So make sure to check the blurb and read along.

Emily Garratt (12)
De Stafford School, Caterham

Burning Fear

I feel alone
afraid and alone.
I cannot seem to open my eyes,
I haven't always been like this.
I guess I'm old and running out of time.

I know they know I'm here,
we watch each other every day,
but I still feel so alone.

They use me but only when they need me,
when they don't I just stand here,
alone and afraid.
I feel neglected.

It's different lately,
I've been here for years,
now I'm getting older,
I'm running out of time.
It's getting shorter,
by the second.

I know I'm still here.
I can see it,
however, my sight is blurred and almost out.
I can feel it.
I just know I'm still here, alive.

I'm nearly gone, so short.
Time is so short.
I can feel myself slowly going,
I wish I had longer.
It's burning me out.
I can't go on anymore.

I can feel it,
I'm going now,
I'm melting,
a candle,
yes, a candle, that's me,
a candle is burning,
now there's nothing left of me.

Evie Lloyd (13)
De Stafford School, Caterham

My Third Eye

With one tap of my phone I reveal my life,
Who knew that one tiny device could open up so many memories?
It has seen so much,
From my favourite places and people and me.

Places is where we start,
There are pictures of different countries like Spain and France,
There's London and the top of the Shard,
And the beaches of Estepona.

My phone has seen people,
My friends, my family, my significant other,
From Sophie to Naima to Bethan to Ivana,
From my mum to my dad or my sister or my brother.

It contains all my favourite and special moments,
It has seen me scoring the winning penalty,
From my first birthday to my fourteenth,
All the parties and sleepovers too.

But most of all it has seen me,
It has seen the real me,
My camera knows how I really am,
Almost as if it's my third eye.

It's seen me dancing and playing about,
It's seen pictures of my favourite people,
It's seen me laugh and it's seen me cry,
And photos and videos of myself and I.

Lily Edwards
De Stafford School, Caterham

Murder In The Amazon

I duck behind a bush,
Trying not to be seen,
The murderer prepares his weapon
And I wonder how someone could be so cruel and mean,
Taking the life of an innocent creature,
Putting the planet in danger,
My breaths get faster and shorter from the fear growing inside me,
I listen to the roar of the machine
I watch the sour look on his face,
Covered by a mask,
I need to do something fast,
But I am too small and weak,
Nothing compares to this hideous beast,
I look around, I need to do something now,
But I don't know what,
I need to do what's right,
I need to put up a fight,
For this place I call home,
But how can I
When I'm weak and alone?
He throws the weapon back,
Preparing for attack,
He stabs the tree in the heart with a knife,

I wish people could realise what's really going wrong and stop this mess,
But sadly that wish will only come true in my head.

Mallory Maguire (13)
De Stafford School, Caterham

Cancer Doesn't Break Me!

Inspired by 'A Monster Calls' by Patrick Ness

As I lie still and fragile in the rock-hard bed,
Terrifying thoughts slip through my head,
Like a boa constrictor around my brain,
It tightens and I feel a pang of pain,
I've seen the tears in Conor's eyes,
And the stone-set face he uses as a disguise,
He knows the future, he is not dumb,
He just never wants the time to come,
I put my hand on my scalp, which is bare,
Oh, how I long to have just one hair,
To cover up all the hurt and pain,
The same treatments that fail and they make me try again,
It could be tomorrow, it could be today,
I know for certain I will pass away,
But even though I will be gone,
I will not be absent for long,
I will come back as a yew tree, proud and strong,
The leaves as my hair, the bark as my dress,
My squirrel children will live in a nest,
I shall live on like the spark in me that shines bright,
That very spark keeps me going for one last night.

Summer Cormack (12)
De Stafford School, Caterham

Once Upon A Stabbing

The cold breeze stroking my face,
The daunting shadows rest on my head,
As I walk down this dark alley place.
A lustrous metal catches the eye,
He sinks it deep through my torso,
As my impotent body flails in the wind.
I find myself in the hospital bed,
Monitors and oxygen sticking from me,
And a sharp pain of fear strikes my head.
I open up the kitchen drawer,
Out comes a lethal blade,
To make sure I don't drop to the floor.
That shadowy figure walks up to me again,
My hand spears it deep through his body,
Then my heart simultaneously fills with shame.
I'm crying alone in my bed,
Wishing I never went near that cursed blade,
Infused with deep dread.
I stand over the towering bridge,
My hands outstretched, grasping it,
Then I once again feel the cold ridge.

Harry Swanson (12)
De Stafford School, Caterham

That's Slightly Out Of Place

That's slightly out of place
Fix it... fix it...
That rug's got all rolled up
Fix it... fix it...
That desk's a mess
Fix it... fix it...
That table isn't parallel with the wall
Fix it... fix it...
That fork isn't straight
Fix it... fix it...
My hands are dirty
Fix it... fix it...
There's dust over there
Fix it... fix it...
Do I smell bad?
Fix it... fix it...
Does my breath stink?
Fix it... fix it...
Have I locked the door?
Fix it... fix it...
Are the windows closed?
Fix it... fix it...
Is my hair a mess?
Fix it... fix it...
That pencil's out of place
Fix it... fix it...

That book should be somewhere else
Fix it... fix it...
That picture's not aligned
Fix it... fix it...
Did I forget something?
Fix it... fix it...
Are my teeth clean?
Fixed it!

Paige Bacon (14)
De Stafford School, Caterham

Grandad

If only I could see you again and tell you how much I cared.
Everything you did for me was never gone unseen.
The world's best grandad, with all the love to give.
Not a single task nor job too much, as you always did.
"Yes," you would say with a smile and a laugh. "Of course I can help you out!"
If only I could see you again to tell you how thankful I am.
I'm so grateful for every single day I got to spend with you.
Life won't be the same again but you are always in my heart.
I look up to the sky at night and see the brightest star shine.
If only I could see you again, the best grandad I will ever have.
You will always remain strong in my heart, as you watch over me I promise to make you proud.
If only I could see you again and tell you how much I cared.

Joshua Walker (12)
De Stafford School, Caterham

Divorce

Tears rolled down my cheeks
They were arguing again
My parents, it had been going on for weeks
They would say they weren't working
Most nights my dad would head to the pub
I couldn't think without my stomach churning
I was lonely so I hugged my pug
I started to think that life was going to get worse
I woke with a start hearing the word 'divorce'
My mind was spinning like having a curse
My thoughts and feelings got all sad
I thought this was because of me
It can't be? I must be going mad!
The room was dark, I could hear my parents outside
They were shouting, but in a whisper
They were saying how much they hated each other and wished they had died
I was on my own, it was quiet and unfamiliar
I could take no more so I closed the door.

Elliot McLaggan (11)
De Stafford School, Caterham

Caged Bird

A person caged, incapsulated,
like a bird caged in a reservation of incapability,
drowning in luminously rusting bars,
under an infinite zenith,
this untangled malformation is perplexingly inaccessible.

Sub-zero conditions become pardoned,
when the activities are consistent of staring,
envisioning imagery of anticipation to juxtapose...

The vast inconveniences and miscalculations in their dexterity,
an archetype in parallel sequences to miscalculations,
they are developed in the minimalism of activities.

I customarily lay, glaring through the luminous rusting bars,
I act as if the compound is translucent,
and I can visualise the malleable welcoming place beyond,
this only lingers and withers the already embryonic emotion.

Markus Nilson (14)
De Stafford School, Caterham

Do I Deserve This?

Lonely. This is what I am,
It's finally getting to me.
It hurts, burns and stings,
All I want is to be set free.

Why? Why does this always happen to me?
All I see is sorrow, madness,
Loneliness and sadness.
Isolation, dreariness everywhere.
Fear and pain all through the air.

Thirteen I am today
Someone please wish me a happy birthday.
What have I done to deserve this?
A tiny piece of cake would be pure bliss.

But I live on the streets,
In my own depressed world
For I have no family, no friends, no home
And also no one to call my own.

Once again to God I shall say
Do I deserve this?
What have I done?
Listen to me, for I pray
To take this horridness away.

Keya Khatri (13)
De Stafford School, Caterham

War

War is a terrible thing
a monster that should be prevented at all costs.

I'm a soldier
standing tall
proud of my uniform
I'm standing, looking at the mess of the place I am in.

The war zone
an unhappy place
full of pain and misery
lifeless bodies all around.

The opposing side
in a deep green uniform
looking like the grass
wait
there is no grass.

All has been destroyed
no one lives here anymore
forced to flee for safety
no animals left
all dead.

War is a terrible thing
it's a monster that should be prevented at all costs.

Tanner Bonds (14)
De Stafford School, Caterham

Icy Chill

A freezing heart, not melted by a soul
Nothing, nothing to make me feel whole
The icy weather creeps unsettling into me
I look down at the ground
What a sight to deceive me
Miles up high, frozen from my head to my toes
Is this the way the story goes?
A whisper, a shriek, I am released
From the hell in the sky
I discover the end is not nigh
I float gently down, I feel so free
So wild and free, that's me
I touch the earth
I cannot be disturbed
But a bright, raging fire looks down from where I began
My heart starts to melt, I'm no longer free
My cold, icy soul is no longer within me.

Rosie Gibbens (12)
De Stafford School, Caterham

Through Their Eyes

Through their eyes, what do they see?
What will they say? What will they do?
Is it dark enough to give someone flu?

In a narrow alleyway, in the middle of the night,
There were two people, their hearts full of fright,
Standing beside the alleyway,
Witnessing it, unable to walk away.

There it was, one armed and one not,
For the fight seemed to last forever,
For neither were very clever.

They fought and fought,
For eternity and beyond,
For neither could do what they had longed.

Through their eyes, what did they see?
For neither can live while the other survives.

Shane Cooper (13)
De Stafford School, Caterham

Falling Tree

I stand tall in a large field
I have bright green leaves on each of my branches
Sometimes the birds come and join me
They sing beautiful songs
I am happy and relaxed
The wind blows fresh air
The sun is shining
But then I grow anxious
I am no longer happy
I am no longer safe
I see something in the distance
A man holding a big axe approaches me
He then starts hitting my legs over and over again
Why do they do this to me?
I help you live
I give you air
But you still abuse me
And push me to the ground
I then stumble to the floor
And now all I am is cut up wood.

Hannah Crutchley (15)
De Stafford School, Caterham

Why Me?

I sit up in bed,
My heart pounding like a speeding bullet,
Tring to keep going,
Telling myself someone cares,
Why me?
Why could it not be someone else?
Why not the person down the street?
Why not the person living next door?
Why me?
Why me?
Why me?
The killer is killing me from the inside out,
The sound of silence is so loud that it blankets everything else out,
I am frightened to leave this world.
Frightened for the suffering my family will be put through when I am not here,
It could have happened to anyone,
All goes dark,
I take my last breath and blow away.

Amy Nash (12)
De Stafford School, Caterham

Subtitles

It's overwhelming sometimes.
The pounding in my head.
The pounding that reminds me what happened.
The pounding that follows me to school every morning,
taunting me.
I try my best to ignore it,
But sometimes I just can't.
It's like trying to ignore subtitles on a screen.
No matter how hard you try not to look at them,
You know they're there.
You know no matter how hard you try you will never forget
their touch.
It haunts you.
It bites away at your hopes for the future,
All you want to do is wake up from this nightmare
But you can't.

Carys Byford (13)
De Stafford School, Caterham

Lost Child

Wandering around the streets, all alone
No food and drink, no mobile phone.

How did I get here? How could this be?
All I want is to be home watching TV.

One stupid argument, one stupid fight
Now that I think of it I might not have been right.

If I go back home and apologise to Mum
My suffering will end and this will all be done.

I open the door, she is there with a smile
She says, "You have been gone for quite a while."

She takes me into her arms as I cry like a baby
She says we might have both been wrong, maybe.

Callum French (12)
De Stafford School, Caterham

The Deep Blue Abyss

The deep blue abyss is where I miss,
On the beach is where I sit,
For I am a whale and have been washed up,
I am tired and covered in muck,
Nobody cares, they won't push,
All of the humans watch from a bush!
"A whale on the land,
How bland!"
"I'll post this on my socials,
I'll show the locals!"
When they felt pain,
I came,
Take me home,
To the love of my life,
Where she is wailing,
Waiting for me to arrive.

Charlotte Groves (12)
De Stafford School, Caterham

Empty

As I lay in my room,
A feeling of numb took over my body
My eyes sleepy and my body disappeared
My arms shaking violently
Curled up in a ball as my brain attacked itself

The light bulb flickered; I longed for it to explode
End my suffering for me, as pathetic for not doing it myself
My mind went blank, empty
Relief flooded through my veins
It suddenly pounced again,
More kicking, scratching and biting
When will it stop?

Chloe E Smith (13)
De Stafford School, Caterham

Voices

Whispers, whispers,
Voices fill my head,
Do this, do that,
Shout what should not be said,
Be happy, be sad,
These voices drive me mad,
She's good, she's bad,
Go away and I'll be glad.

Go up, no, go down,
Smile, now frown,
Stand still, spin around,
Don't stop until you hit the ground,
I'm trapped, can't hide,
The voices never leave my mind.

Hollie Rubhunya (13)
De Stafford School, Caterham

Colourless

Black and white
Everybody colourless
Watching TV as if it's the 60s
Does everyone else see the same?
Black and white

The green of the trees
Black and white

The deep blue ocean
Black and white

Some kind of haze covers my eyes
Unable to see the colours of the world
Black and white

All I have ever known.

Katie Bacon (14)
De Stafford School, Caterham

Connor Mcgregor

Surprise, surprise, the king is back
It only took 40 seconds for Cerone to get a smack
Like the fight, this is going too quick
I will put you to the ground with a head kick
Then I will hit you with a left
You'll hit me with a right
Either way, you'll go night-night
This is a quick match, this one on one
We now have the notorious one!

Ollie Moroney (15)
De Stafford School, Caterham

The Bottle

Bang, bang, bang
went the bottle as the cap burst open
Fizz, fizz, fizz
went the bubbles shooting out of me
Wet, wet, wet
as my jacket became drenched
Silly, silly, silly
how silly can I be?

Shaking the bottle
Letting the bubbles free
All over me!

Zac Baker (11)
De Stafford School, Caterham

The Creature In The Woods

Everyone fears me
And people say they should
But if they just got to know me
They would see that I am good
I don't harm anyone
Not even the wood!
I wish I had a friend
I want one so bad
I hope someone will lend a helping hand
I don't know why I am feeling so sad.

Ethan Sewell (13)
De Stafford School, Caterham

The Minotaur

Inspired by Carol Ann Duffy

Shame.
A familiar feeling.
Born as a mistake.
A form of disgust to take.

Run.
Anger is a lesson taught.
Love can't help but hide.
Fear grows from the inside.

Forget.
I am what you made me.
The fire that burns within me,
Is one sparked by your apathy.

One life.
Two life.
Three life.
Dead.
Blood on my hands,
Falls on your head.

Another.
Men aren't brave.
He acts not on justice,
But so others call him selfless.

Take.
Take my life because you can.
Maybe there is good in what you do.
Save me from the men like you.

I am what you made me.
Take the life they regret they gave me.

Lauren Wright
East Norfolk Sixth Form College, Gorleston

Mrs Bundy

Inspired by Carol Ann Duffy

To all those tormented souls,
How could these events be?
Each of you had your goals,
Obstructed by my dearest Teddy.
Destruction. Desolation. Damage. Despair.
Oblivious you were to your fate,
Rushed was your claret hair
Examine his work: Theodore the Great.

Ella Loades & Megan Hall
East Norfolk Sixth Form College, Gorleston

The Destruction Of Knowledge

Some poems are funny
Some are profane
But this is my story
A story of pain...

War was announced upon our country
Scrambling, dashing, we made our way to the border
Only to be met with guns, soldiers and many more deadly weapons
We swiftly turned back on ourselves like timid mice
Bang! Bang! Bang! was all ringing through my ears
As I stared in horror at the tragic scenes unfolding
These people, friends, family and more, people who I had known for years
Were falling to the ground like chopped down trees
All my years in this pretty village were being torn apart
Ruined by this act of out of order behaviour
Why? I asked
Why do we need to fight?
Why is one problem spinning into an uncontrolled bloodbath?
The answer I felt was not there
There was no way to stop this
That's when they turned on me, the village elder
107 years of wisdom, destroyed by two single bullets
One to the heart and one to the head.

Sam Elves (13)
Farringdon Community Academy, Farringdon

Climate Change

What a beautiful day in New York City,
The sky is grey and that's a pity.
A group of small humans stop by,
But eventually wave their friends goodbye.
A typical day in the life of a building,
Watching families walk by with their children.
But wait, what's that sound?
There is a lot of water on the ground!
It won't stop, it can't stop, it won't go away,
I'm afraid it is here to stay.
Something is really not right, the clouds are crying,
There's too much water, the sea levels are rising.
Everyone's screaming and people are dying,
Other buildings are falling, this is terrifying!
I think I am falling, I don't know what to do,
Water is all I can see in my field of view!
Help, help, help, help!

What a beautiful day in an Australian town,
It's very hot and it makes me frown.
I wonder what today will be like,
I see a lot of humans riding on bikes.
Just a typical day in the life of a building,
Watching families run away with their children.
But what's that? What's that smell?
Some trees in the distance just fell!

I see some orange sparks far away,
Where are all the humans today?
I fear the humans know something, something that is now coming,
My situation seems very dire, wait a moment, could that be... fire?
The sun is too hot, everything is burning,
It's getting closer and closer and my stomach is churning.
Everything around me is going down in flames,
All of my friends are in so much pain!
Why aren't people trying to stop it?
The world is falling apart bit by bit!
Fire, fire, fire, fire!

Harrison Colley (12)
Farringdon Community Academy, Farringdon

The Pile

Piled up
up and up
like a colossal weight of paper
layer upon layer
dragging me down
a hold by the neck.

With every breath
a thread slipped away
at the seams
just like that
every second wasted
simply 'cause the pen was too lazy.

In the depths
lungs mingled with liquid
the little words present
locked away
held captive in the throat
scraping claws, nails, knives
at the vocal cords
screaming with no vibration.

Slowly
slow like a puncture
silence ringing
suffocating
the crisp, cream pile and the black ballpoint

the last stop
the final moment
and the breaking point.

The pile
it was too much
too large
it was only time
before it fell
fell for good
dashed to pieces
yet somehow
by some magic
it always came back.

Victoria Rooks (15)
Farringdon Community Academy, Farringdon

Dog's Life

I am a dog and my name is Anna,
I am different from every dog but I don't care,
I get chased a lot by the most popular dogs,
My owner loves me a lot but is always at work.

When I go outside the other dogs try to attack,
My owner gets very mad, very fast,
She takes me inside, away from the others,
My owner is just like my mother.

I hate being around other dogs,
The dogs hate me and this is my doggy life,
The story behind all this hatred is very simple,
It all started when I was alone in my garden,
I then saw a dog and got all excited,
Then the dog started to bark in an angry way.

Ever since then I won't interact with another dog,
I am now very sad,
My owner is very mad.

My message for this poem is: Don't treat others any different.

Chloe Hutchinson (12)
Farringdon Community Academy, Farringdon

Deforestation

The people march in again and again,
My forest is turning into ash in a second.
The sound of the wood crashing to the floor,
It's enough to send anyone away far.

Most of my family have already left,
Except me as my time still hasn't come.,
Hopefully soon I will be blessed,
As I can't bear to live in this ash anymore.

My home is gone,
And the trees with it too.
If I'm not stopped soon,
I'm sure I will go with it.

All of my prey went with it,
Maybe I'll starve and be saved from depression.
The men no longer come as there is nothing left to chop,
Wood wasted on people who didn't need it.

Greed overtook,
Now look where it has got us.
Innocents dying every second,
Because of the humans destroying the planet!

Jessica Hibberd (12)
Farringdon Community Academy, Farringdon

I Feel Something Approaching

I feel something approaching
It knows I am here
Lost in the mist, overpowering the darkness
It creeps around almost silently
As I look around with blueish eyes, lighting up the darkness

I hear something approaching
It sneaks around as if I am its prey
I nervously walk through the dark snow
It stalks me as I move

I know something is approaching
It probably hears my movement in the crunching of the snow
The sound of my jacket rubbing on my clothes
I feel like I am getting nervous to breathe
As crazy as someone in a mental asylum

It is approaching
It is studying how I move
It comes closer
It knows I hear it
It sees me move faster
It catches up
I am now it
I am the one approaching…

Thomas Marshall (13)
Farringdon Community Academy, Farringdon

Dark And Dirty Place

My mind is very close to death
And in this dark place I cannot even take a breath
My lungs are filled to the chest
I'm isolated behind these forbidden bars
Lonely, depressed, but I am no different to the rest
They all think this is hell, there is no place to be happy
I walk with my cuffs strapped to my wrist
There is no light inside, just blackness
The building is a soulless prison
It can break people mentally and scar them for life
It is enough to make a grown man cry
I am filthy, haven't had a shower in years
I am missing my family, this always has me in tears
The person who put me here should be ashamed
I don't even know what normal life is like
But according to statistics, I should be inside.

Logan Tayim (12)
Farringdon Community Academy, Farringdon

Deforestation

I feel as though my world is collapsing,
As I open my eyes to this wreck of a forest,
The grass, no trees, nowhere to go.
I sit alone in the Devil's garden,
Imagining what it once was,
The trees, the life, the happiness.
They took my happiness, they took my home,
I don't know what I have done to deserve this,
But they didn't care, they didn't think,
For someone like me.
All of a sudden red flames appear,
Big mechanical monsters are chasing me,
I scream and shout for help but no one seems to hear.
They just carry on making me live in fear,
I am alone,
And forever will be now, no one is here,
I'm just another problem.

Bayleigh Maughan (11)
Farringdon Community Academy, Farringdon

A Prisoner In My Own Body

I was once a prisoner in my own body,
Flooded in my thoughts and feelings,
I couldn't see, I could only hear,
But no one was even about.

I was screaming all day,
I was screaming all night,
But no one was around to hear me shout.

One day I heard a voice,
They called me worthless,
And left me with my thoughts.

I didn't hear any nice thoughts for a long, long time,
And then I was told he will die,
When I heard I screamed and I cried,
But I didn't make a sound.

I heard a voice that I seemed to know,
It was my beloved father and I began to remember,
I wasn't stuck,
I trapped myself...

Ben Williams (11)
Farringdon Community Academy, Farringdon

Two Parents

Two parents, two parents who love me
But only one loves the other
Held together like a piece of string
A very thin piece of string that is slowly snapping with each day
That piece of string is me

Two parents, two parents who love me but know things won't last
Arguing and fighting constantly
I become aware of this nightmare and am losing hope

Two parents, two parents who love me but still I wonder where it went wrong
I wonder how I went from everything to nothing but disappointment

One parent, one parent who truly loves me
One single parent who will struggle forever
But what a bummer
But, oh well, I got a free Hummer.

Ryan Soper (13)
Farringdon Community Academy, Farringdon

The Last And First Light

As I stood in the cold
I could see everything
Some sad, some happy
But this time it was sad

As a street light people think I have no emotion
But this time the rain ran down me like a tear running down my face
I see people's first hours on Earth
But this time I saw someone's last

As they rushed out of the house
It was hard to see
But I knew
It was someone's last hours on Earth

That friendly chap down the street
No longer there
That friendly chap down the street
Is now in another place

But this time I knew
I would see them again
As I saw them walking to the gates of Heaven.

Matthew Crabtree (14)
Farringdon Community Academy, Farringdon

I Am In Pain

As the tears run down my face
I am sat in the corner while it pours with rain
People walk past me at a regular pace
But they don't see me sitting in the rain

No one bothers to help
I cannot scream or yelp
I'm left sitting on the street
With people walking past that don't see me on the street

When people walk past I beg
For some food or just an egg
I say, "It's my life at risk!"
However, they carry on as if it's them that is at risk

I am not a master of disguise
I know they can see it in my eyes
But they choose to leave me in pain
For I am in pain...

Ruby Large (12)
Farringdon Community Academy, Farringdon

My Walk In The Park

I am woken in the morning
All snuggled in bed
As my human comes to greet me
And pats me on the head
It's time to munch my breakfast
But once I have finished eating
My owner shouts, "Walkies!"
I wonder who I'll be meeting
Walking down the street
With the wind blowing through my fur
I look up and think
I love walks out with her
As we walk a little further
We'll soon be at the park
I can't stop my tail from wagging
And I give a little bark
I spot my friend the Labrador
We sniff and say hello
Running laps around the field
But now it's time to go.

Heidi Smith (11)
Farringdon Community Academy, Farringdon

The Ocean

There's plastic in the ocean,
The turtles cry in pain,
Can holders wrapped around their shells,
It's driving them insane.

There's plastic in the ocean,
The octopi try and escape,
Little do they know though,
Their home will never be the same.

There's plastic in the ocean,
The whales are slowly dying,
Because their diet isn't normal,
Their calls to each other sound like crying.

There's plastic in the ocean,
It's causing climate change,
The planet is being killed by greenhouse gasses,
Plastic must be recycled by the masses.

Freya Nichol (12)
Farringdon Community Academy, Farringdon

Mental Health

Why can't you see me the way I see myself
I am trapped and alone, crying in my home

The thoughts in my head are telling me to go
But I know that I can't, I am about to blow

I try to move on but they just won't let go
Why can't you see me this hurt and alone?

This fame and success isn't the best
For these thoughts in my head I need to rest
This harsh life of mine is putting me to the test

Mental health isn't the best
I can't just put it to the side to rest
They say go and get help and not be depressed!

Deyanna Robinson (13)
Farringdon Community Academy, Farringdon

No-Man's-Land

I stood frozen,
Frightened throughout,
The sounds of the guns and shells,
Battered my ears.

I looked around for a moment,
Around the dark, dirty trench,
To watch my best friend,
Be blown to smithereens.

It was like watching a china plate smash,
His body in 100 pieces,
I knew as I saw him die,
It was his time to go,
My time to go on to...
No-man's-land.

I climbed up the trench ladder,
Frightened, honoured,
And I knew what happened,
I was prepared to die.

To die on
No-man's-land.

Charlie Gettins (13)
Farringdon Community Academy, Farringdon

Framed And Empty

I have been here too long feeling sad
I have been missing my mum and dad
I have started to forget my past
I don't know how long my memory will last
I don't know how long I will be here
I just hope I can hold my family near
I miss my wife and my daughter
I hope they are all right
I miss telling my child goodnight
As long as they are safe at home
That is all I really need to know
I am feeling empty inside
I told the jury I was framed and I cried
They didn't believe me and now I am here
Rotting in a cell and waiting to see her.

Zac Schonewald (12)
Farringdon Community Academy, Farringdon

Going For Gold

Last week a letter came through the door
I read it and fell to the floor
Tears of happiness flooded down my face
It said: 'You have been chosen by the Olympics to run a race'

Every day I work hard while I train
Trying to concentrate on the goal, not the pain
Always getting drenched in sweat
Hoping the other people are not a threat

All of my family are so proud of me
But will I succeed? We will have to wait and see
When the day arrives will I crumble and fold
Or will I be standing on the podium holding the gold?

Anna Gaffney (12)
Farringdon Community Academy, Farringdon

I Finally Saw Him

I felt myself falling
It finally came to an end
I opened my eyes
Got up
That's when I saw him

He then saw me and smiled
He ran over to me like a dart
Oh how he looked so smart
I saw him

We played and talked for hours
He gave me some flowers
Oh how I missed you
I saw him

Grampa was my world
But he was taken
Oh how cruel
But I saw him

In the blink of an eye
He was gone again
I wasn't in the same room
Oh no, he was gone again
I no longer see him.

Tamzin Facey (14)
Farringdon Community Academy, Farringdon

The Environment Experience

The trees up high as monkeys swing
But down below the birds sing
The plants grow quietly and slowly
As the waves howl at the silent moon

Slowly the pandas come out of their domain
Shouting and wincing in pain
Animals shouting and crying for help
Nobody comes, nobody hears the yelp

I go and say, "What's wrong?"
A huge tree falls on a baby tiger's home
A loud chainsaw is heard in the distance chopping down animal's homes
Animals dying of hunger and pain
Once a rainforest
Now a desert!

Ben Howe (12)
Farringdon Community Academy, Farringdon

The Life Of Anne Frank

Today was scary
I thought I was going to be caught
I heard someone outside
I prayed to God
That today was not the day
The day the Nazis would come
The day I would be taken away
The day that could be my last
The day that I could only be with my family
For the very last time

I felt like my heart was in my mouth
My hands were clenched onto my mam's
I thought of the very worst every single day
But luckily it wasn't
I was relieved
I was jumping for joy
But just inside so no one could hear us!

Daynie Yeates (13)
Farringdon Community Academy, Farringdon

Dark Place

In this dark and dirty place
Something I can't face
Inside of me I know I should be here
But I couldn't be here, even for my biggest fear
I miss my family, I just want to go home
Because this isn't the place for me
I know I have been framed
And the person who leads this should be ashamed

I don't know my sentence
Hopefully, it won't be long because I know my daughter will be wondering when Daddy will be home
My mind is very close to death
And in this dark place I cannot find my breath.

Harley Waites (12)
Farringdon Community Academy, Farringdon

The Lottery

If I won the lottery
I would buy 10 cars
I would get 1,000 golden chains.

I would lie on my back
And look at the stars in my observatory
I would buy.

While eating my golden
Steak I would give
A free house
To anybody.

I would drop the bomb
On the news
When they found out I
was planning to travel the world in a golden
Boat!

My family's brains
Would come out of their ears
When I bought them all houses
But this is all just a dream.

Jacob Kay (12)
Farringdon Community Academy, Farringdon

I Have A Secret

I have a secret
and that is true
I have a secret
that I want to release to you

The secret is special
so I'm only telling a few
and I will release it to the world
but only with the help of you

I wish to tell my parents
I wish it was as easy as serving it on a tray
but the truth is
that I am gay

But if I release this on social media
chaos could ensue
I could get bullied
my life could be ruined by only a small few...

Josh Campbell (13)
Farringdon Community Academy, Farringdon

It Is Pain

It is pain
My fingers turning to ice
Death blowing wind hitting me against my head
I am not wanted

It is pain
No one really listens
I have no one
I have been judged

It is pain
I have nothing
I am always alone in the dark
My clothes scare everyone like a crow

It is pain
Every day is like a living nightmare
The rain cries along with me
I want something better
I need something better
Please, please, please.

Lili Farina (12)
Farringdon Community Academy, Farringdon

The Same As You

As I am walking down the street,
no shoes on my feet.
I see the glares of disgust,
there is no one to trust.

I'm looking at my skin,
you make me feel like a sin.
Yet I am the same as you,
but different nonetheless.

You're calling me names,
like it's one of your games.
But it isn't a game,
you're saying it again.

You laugh at me,
you mock me.
Yet we are the same,
but different nonetheless.

Grace Terry (11)
Farringdon Community Academy, Farringdon

A Mental Prisoner

A mental prisoner,
yes, that is me,
stuck in my own body,
it's not who I want to be.

A mental prisoner,
I have no choice,
all I hear is that one voice,
saying that I am not good enough.

A mental prisoner,
shy and timid,
not a word comes out of me,
that's why I'm scared.

A mental prisoner,
what's the point of living?
If only others knew how I felt,
maybe then I would be okay.

Beki Wild (12)
Farringdon Community Academy, Farringdon

The Ups And Downs

I am a slide in a nice place
The laughter I hear puts a smile on me
Everything I know is when the light runs down on me and I wait
I wait for voices and it always pays off
Because I hear giggles and I love that.

The big and small ones all talk about their lives
Who they are with and it is nice
But for the longest time I have been like this
They never come back at some point.
But the laughter, I love it
I truly do.

Rhys Thompson (14)
Farringdon Community Academy, Farringdon

Mercy

I am Mercy
I'm the one
Who will save you
From the gun

Or the electric chair
Or the needle
That's not fair
You're irreplaceable

Have mercy on this man
Have mercy on his soul
His skin may be black
But his life you have stole

Don't come to me
When those of colour are extinct
Between all humanity
There is a link

Dear police officer
Have mercy...

Anton Haley (11)
Farringdon Community Academy, Farringdon

Havoc On Earth

They cut my trees so I can no longer climb
Imagine that
They strike me down to make paper
Imagine that
My ground is melting
Imagine that
It's your fault
Imagine that
You can cut my horns off
Imagine that
You can kill me for them
Imagine that
You hurt me
Imagine that
You turn a blind eye and ignore us
Imagine that
Now this is our last cry
Imagine that
Imagine that...

Phoebe Croniin (11)
Farringdon Community Academy, Farringdon

Bullying

White, black
it doesn't matter
you are you
girls get judged for wanting to be boys
boys get judged for wearing make-up and girl's clothing
to this day people still get bullied for what they look like and what size they are
it needs to stop
it is going too far
how would you like it if you got bullied for the way you look?
Think everyone is perfect, including you
so what we need to do is stop bullying.

Maddison Marsh (11)
Farringdon Community Academy, Farringdon

The Problem Of Sexuality

The voices argue back and forth,
my life feels like it is breaking apart.
No one to tell, nothing to say
I cannot tell people I am gay.

My life feels like it's breaking in half,
my heart feels like it is sawn in half
No one to see, nothing to say,
I just have to get through the day.

My parent don't know, my friends nether
but I don't want to come out of the closet either!

Ben Hanson (13)
Farringdon Community Academy, Farringdon

Youth Club

It's Friday night, it's youth club tonight
It's a chance to hit the pitch, with my friend Mitch.
Running with the ball, no need to feel tall
Doing a trick, may take the mick

Many different balls bouncing off the walls
Might be offside, but you tried.
When it gets dark, we leave the park
It's only a short walk, no need to joke.

Patrick Gokcan (11)
Farringdon Community Academy, Farringdon

Death Row

Alone in my cell
Thoughts about my execution
It's too late for regrets
I am living my last days
Soon I will breathe my last breath
I think hardly about what I will eat for my last meal
I wonder every day if I will be executed
Or if I will be set free from this torture
Wondering if I can escape this nightmare
Soon I will find out...

Ian Gage (12)
Farringdon Community Academy, Farringdon

Timothy Winters

I am the colour grey,
No one hears as the sad music plays,
As I lay in sadness every other day,
Lonely as can be but nothing else to say,
Every time I get dosed with aspirin
Don't know what to do, no way
Don't know where to stay,
On the floor is where I lay,
I only want to play,
But hey, only if I could sway.

Sophie Chapman (11)
Farringdon Community Academy, Farringdon

Nature's Truth

The burning trees
The crying bees
But what are we doing to stop it?
Nothing
You can make a difference
So do it
Look what you are doing to your children's future
Animals are becoming extinct
Because of you
Change
Change the way you live
Recycle, reuse
It all helps
Change for a better future.

Darcie Taylor (13)
Farringdon Community Academy, Farringdon

On The Darkest Of Days

I am a pain,
I am never happy,
I am always in the rain,
I never see the sun,
It's always dark and dull,
I walk around the streets, no one to say hello,
I lay in bed on the darkest day watching the wind blow,
Why is it always me
Lying there asleep
Just on the darkest of days?

Kaitlyn McNeil (12)
Farringdon Community Academy, Farringdon

Banter

Banter
When everyone laughs
Banter
When no one cries
Banter
Not bullying
Banter
Slowly killing people
Banter
Turns into bullying
Banter
Leads to self-harm
Banter
It is all around
Banter
Don't turn it into bullying!

Sophie Collins (11)
Farringdon Community Academy, Farringdon

The Piano

I am a piano
My keys are black and white
When you start to press them
My music is a delight
Inside me are little hammers that hit upon the strings
When you start to play me
The music, it begins.

Dillan Howarth (11)
Farringdon Community Academy, Farringdon

World War II - Two Lost Hearts

Away in the distance over there,
Lies a war before us full of hatred and fear
Every single soul fighting for liberation,
Seeks only one thing which is to go back and find that same devotion

How he missed his grandma's embrace,
Takes him back to that same place
Where he would hear the chirping of birds all day long,
And he would also take the urge to sing along
Laughing and giggling through adventures he would face,
Reminded him of the happiness he would chase

His grandma yearning day and night,
For the sparkle of her life to come back alright
Bless these souls, oh mighty Lord,
And reunite them to the love they have lost...

Khairun Nessa Momo (12)
Kantor King Solomon High School, Barkingside

The Death Upon Loved Ones

The death upon you
It hits you at random
You will never know when
It will catch you

Don't think I'm joking
Because I'm not
It hit my loved ones...
I'm still not joking

Donate to cancer
To help it die

One thing you don't notice
I am what's harming people
I am cancer and I need stopping
It's in my blood
It's not like I want to hurt people for a living
Please don't blame me
Just donate to Cancer Research UK to kill me today!

Zak Cohen (11)
Kantor King Solomon High School, Barkingside

Environmental Poem

The wonderful world, please just try to survive
As people destroy you day by day
We shall stand before you, to try keep you alive

Help the world survive
Don't use single-use plastic for foods
Buy, use reusable pots
Don't litter
For the extra minute it takes
Put it in the bin
Any food waste created
Lives better in a compost bin
Than all over the floor

Save our animals
Save our people
Save our generation
Save the world around us.

Rosie Preston (12)
Kantor King Solomon High School, Barkingside

Through The Years

A spark of life, deep in my ocean
A blink of an eye, now they have motion
Now they're evolving, moving out of the sea
Developing eyes to look at me
T-rex walk, pterodactyl fly
But oh no, what's that high in the sky?
Asteroid hitting me, what a disaster
Dinosaurs gone, who's my new master?
Monkeys and apes swing through the trees
Then they discover fire burning me
Digging into my depths, breaking my skin
Mining me out, everything from within
Creating machines, polluting my surface
Then trying to stop it in a deadly race
I am feeling faint, I am too hot
And they are too late, too late by a lot
My vision is dark, this is the end
But now it is too late to mend
I take one last breath and sigh
They have betrayed me and now I must die.

Niamh Taylor (13)
St John's Marlborough, Marlborough

An End

Don't forget about me,
I'm still here
just waiting
for you
everyone
to finish
but no need to fear
I won't hurt but I can
you can make me hurt
I'm on the edge, the point
the top, the cusp
the boundary, the extent
I'm a deadline
and end
the end
all good things come to an end
good things...
all good things?
But not bad?
Not bad
pain, hurt
devastation
they don't
won't end
they aren't god
death

that won't end
I will be there
behind you
this will end
that will end
you will end
and when it does
I will be fed
the end
I strive for the end
any end
the irony though
the end
can't
won't
ever
end
no, the end can't end
I feel one coming
I'm hungry for an end
but things can't start without
an end
a book
a line
a building
a light
the dark

darkness in an end
to a lot of things
although nothing
is an end to but one thing
that's
us
we
you
him
her
she
he
they
all
nothing
like
the world
Earth
the universe
they started
they can end
I can't wait
I'm excited
I'm still here
don't forget
always
now

it's time
I lick my lips
ready
I can taste
the
end.

George Shepard (14)
St John's Marlborough, Marlborough

The Day Before The War

Just before the war,
I was a normal child,
Never had a care in the world,
I was actually happy for a while,
But that was the day before the war.

Now I look at other children,
Just beyond the bars,
Hoping that maybe one day,
I could be as happy as they are.

They treat us like we are obnoxious rodents,
Carrying a disease,
They torture us every day,
No matter how much we plead.

One day my daddy went for a shower,
His clothes joined the stack,
But day by day the pile grows,
And nobody comes back.

What makes me different to other children?
My race?
My colour?
Just because I'm in a striped uniform,
Does it make me a monster to any other?

Now I sit here writing this poem,
Not going through pain anymore,
But I want to let everyone know what life was like,
The day before the war.

Cerian Davies (12)
St John's Marlborough, Marlborough

All Alone

As I open my eyes and see a world of hate
I lie on the ground these cruel humans create
My paws are wet and my ears are soggy
And the people who walk past say, "Poor little doggy!"
But no one really cares, they leave me alone
Oh, please, someone take me home

I don't know how many more days I can last
I'm not sure but I think my life has passed
I have no one, I'm not cheerful
My life is dull and I am fearful

My body is aching, it's so racked with pain
And I pray to God, it won't rain
The people chase me with stones and leave me
Just skin and bone

If I die before I wake
I pray one hopeless should God will take
My tears have gone, my faith is bare
Lord, please hear my rescue prayer.

Emily Lappin (13)
St John's Marlborough, Marlborough

Trapped

I'm just a kid like any other
I am only ten and have two younger brothers
My life is very different to yours
No welcoming arms, no open doors

I really want to go back to school
To see other children, big or small
Instead I'm stuck here in this camp
It's cold, dark and very damp
I don't know how long
I will be trapped here for
It feels so wrong

I wish I could go back to my old life
To escape the guns
To escape the knives

They say 'There's no place like home'
Without it, I've never felt more alone
Why can't I get away from all the dying?
When will I ever stop crying?

Daisy Fry (13)
St John's Marlborough, Marlborough

A Rubik's Cube

I am nice and fidgety,
I am fun to play with,
I can make people rage,
Even when they have success!

They are happy,
I have six faces,
On each face,
I have nine parts.

You try,
And try,
And try,
And try.

You solve one side,
You do it again,
You find a different side,
But destroy the original.

When people get close to solving me,
They rush,
They fail,
They rage and throw me in the bin.

Others take time and are patient,
They succeed in solving me,
They tell their friends,
And the owner presets me.

Their friends congratulate them
They ask for help,
To solve me.

Lin Jun Zheng (12)
St John's Marlborough, Marlborough

A Sunny Day Covers It Up

If a turtle died in the sea,
Would you know?
Or would you still
Be playing in the sand,
Because everything is fine on the land?

If plastic killed a tiny seal pup,
Nobody would care.
Because a sunny day
Covers it up.

As long as there is fun,
Nobody would know.
How could they?
They just want to have fun, then go.

As long as there's a blue sky,
All of the fish can die.

The day is hot,
Sunny on the beach.
But plastic takes fishes' lives
Like a leech.

If plastic killed a tiny seal pup,
Nobody would care.
A sunny day always covers it up.

Sachen Heer
St John's Marlborough, Marlborough

Control

It's weird, isn't it,
When you've broken the atmosphere,
Nothing to hold you back?
Split the sky in half,
Go further than the limit,
Open your eyes,
Too much of a surprise,
Hypnotised once you have seen it.
You can go anywhere, do anything,
No boundaries,
No gates,
No longer in the confinement of your world,
You're free,
Otherworldly,
You control your fate,
Where shall you go?
Nobody knows,
You don't even know what is happening or where you are,
Try and think of something,
Make the sky fall if you want,
Create a stage show
And you'll be the star.

Oscar Holmes (12)
St John's Marlborough, Marlborough

The Unspeakable Nightmare

Crimson flags flutter in the gale,
In the distant path of my gaze,
Plumes of death are impelled into a trail,
As my face turns ashen and pale,
To see the golden stars upon one's heart, beside me,
From a vast and bloody maze.

Screeching sirens rattle through the empty shells
That once stood as someone's home,
Billows of smoke arrive in plumes
Yet still, I lay alone.

An ebony sea floods the sky,
Washing over the pitiful sight that lies below,
The ghastly day ends,
To begin the night,
It is only the sun that has set,
But this unspeakable nightmare shall stay for life.

Evie Mundy (13)
St John's Marlborough, Marlborough

My War Boy

It's war again,
Time and time again,
I served for four years,
And soon my son will go,
Feel my feelings,
Hear my thoughts,
See our loved ones die in our arms,
Like I did...

I felt my heart throbbing out my chest.
Bombs flying through the battlefield,
Endless explosions blurred my senses
All I heard were screams of fear;
All I felt was loneliness;
All I saw was scarlet-red blood, flooding the seas of war.
I wanted to forget the sea of pain.
After becoming a ghost; after the field of vain.

It's time for my boy to go...
Goodbye, my war boy...

Fonteyn Ip (14)
St John's Marlborough, Marlborough

Captive

Eloquent? Not I
Fancy word that my
English dictionary taught to me
I have been here for but three
Decades but it feels closer to a century

They hound me, my dreams
Not a crumb to eat, not even sour cream
They hold me here day and day
Hoping it will end, I pray

They squeeze us for information
About where I was upon my station
No more are my friends
I hope I'm not chosen, or here it ends

Away, away, now I must go
Else I'll get caught, I don't want that, no
This shan't be the last, I shall cope
At least, I hope...

Guy Sainsbury (12)
St John's Marlborough, Marlborough

War Horse, I Am

War...
Here I am again.
Why? No one wanted this, nor did I.
So innocent
Yet...

Nothing will be the same, I panic, I fear, I run.
Non-stop bombing, no one will stop.
No peace,
No mercy.
Sacrifice is made and hatred does arise.
Battlefields for miles
I run and I run.
When can I stop?
When will I stop?

Panic, fear, easy turn to death.
I didn't ask for this,
Yet, I still run.
They won't stop,
Not until one side drops.
Gunshot, bomb-landing
Heart pounding, blood.
And still,
I run and I run.

Jia-Ling Yu (14)
St John's Marlborough, Marlborough

Space Dust

Vroom!
The NASA rocket landed on the desolate wasteland
A world consumed by time
Engines slowing, excited cheers
The expedition has begun
Slow footsteps dusting the rocky wasteland
Heavy breathing, heart pumping
The roar and hum of the Rover, the marks in the sand
Samples of rock being taken to the base for set up
Tonight's food: a mushy packet of slop - at least I have got my crew
Days pass, sleepless nights, the whole nation watching
Departure day - mission complete, ready to lift off and go
Leaving the planet of Mars, ready for the long journey home.

Jacob Smith (13)
St John's Marlborough, Marlborough

Rejected
The point of view of an idea

I spark to life in her head,
The idea that the dead aren't really dead.
I cartwheel around, ticking clogs,
Wheezing smoke, a catalogue.
Full of phrases, stanzas and all,
Watch me bounce, watch me sprawl.
On the floor, where I stay,
Someone new has come to play.
Bigger, better, bolder, brighter,
The idea that ice could come out lighter.
It's so much better, phasing a rainbow,
It hits me like a wooden crossbow.
I am forgotten, I am lost,
The unselected, the tossed.
For I am rejected, hear me scream,
I'll sit here sobbing, spouting steam.

Madeline Wood (13)
St John's Marlborough, Marlborough

Perfect

The world could be perfect
The world should be
The world could be silent
The world should be

One word wouldn't ripple water
Even if it did no one would care
One word could make a difference
Perfect is still, unalive

Who would know
What it feels like?
Who should know
The future from the past?

No one needs to move
There's nothing to promote
No one cares
Attention is not needed, wanted

Everything is a statue
No ideas are allowed to move
That's me. Perfect
A never-changing doll.

Imogen Carter (12)
St John's Marlborough, Marlborough

A Poem

I keep law and order
I am the only thing that drives the world
I allow humans to comprehend the universe
But am never thanked

I'm the force that drives your car
Train or bike
I allow lanes to take flight
But am never thanked

I allow the food that you eat to be eaten
The air that you breathe to breathe
The water that you drink to be taken
But you never thank me

You praise your ethereal god
You thank the wind and the breeze
You thank all but one
You never thank me

I am Science.

Alex Hawtin (14)
St John's Marlborough, Marlborough

Prison Guard

I hate my life,
So full of strife.

Day by day,
It has to pay.

This misery, this guilt, this expected disdain,
Stabs into me like the harshest pain.

Prisoners, here, there and everywhere,
Trudging along the pleading
How do they live?
What can I give
To aid these poor souls,
To fill their empty holes?

They have done wrong, no doubt,
But what is wrong with smiling when I am about?

Sprinkling sugar on their gruel,
Just making their lives a little less cruel.

Sophie Elvey (12)
St John's Marlborough, Marlborough

All I Do Is Tick

It's lonely being Time
All I do is simply tick
And it hurts when they exclaim
"The time has gone too quick!"
I am terribly sorry
And it makes me want to scream
When the night comes to an end
And I cut off your child's dream
But I shall keep ticking
I will wave as the days go by
And close my ears to the horrific sound
Of a newborn baby's cry
So you should thank me really
For the new chances I bring
And for the vibrant fuchsias
That say hello in the spring.

Thea Wratten (12)
St John's Marlborough, Marlborough

Unwanted

Imprisoned day after day
I no longer have anything
hour after hour
all my kings are banishing

I try to be happy
but have to wait quietly
cannot talk, not even to myself
just sit there trying not to think about my health

The days are long
no food to go around
they believe I am wrong
they all want me drowned
while they watch and crown

They treat me like a hound
and don't want me around
I feel no longer wanted
and am constantly hunted.

Sian Hampshire (13)
St John's Marlborough, Marlborough

Need

Another culprit captured.
Hungry rib cages escape his constricted skin.
Giant spirals inside of me; my truth exposed.
So simple, yet too simple, his life
Trapped within my barricades of hunger…

My walls of termination
His skin anticipating darkness
Crumpling, shrivelling, facing the ongoing threat of Death.

Until finally, after balloon-bellied pain;
Despair and eternal adversary,
Death imprisons his childhood.
Loss because of my greedy, selfish ways.

Lucy Bartlett (13)
St John's Marlborough, Marlborough

Climate War

I'm big, I'm scary but you created me
Habitats are destroyed by you, not me
God gave you the world but you created me
Now I am here to stay but you can't solve my puzzles
Now people like Greta warn of my chaos
I'm not a laughing matter
The extinction rate is going through the roof
My dear sorrowful humans
I did not mean to start the bush fires
You forced me to do that
Now you have learnt your lesson
I have to go and stop you making me pollute the world.

Ollie Watson (11)
St John's Marlborough, Marlborough

Last Minutes

I picked up my metal fork and knife,
And I realised this was the end of my life,
I tasted the food, so delicious and sweet
And I realised this was my final treat.

*I'm not supposed to be here, I did nothing wrong,
There is another man who isn't where he belongs,*
I sat in the chair with this thought in my head
Ten seconds later, I'm completely dead.

I close my eyes, I'm fading away
At least now I'll be in a better place.

Archie Balsdon (13)
St John's Marlborough, Marlborough

The Race

The adrenaline, the rush went to my head,
A couple of tons underneath me was lead,
Into the stalls and she stretched out her head,
Her hooves rushed in a blur,
The race began to see what she was worth,
Her pounding heart was working hard,
And I raised the whip like a sword,
This was it, the final furlong,
We were running along,
That was it, we had won,
At last, I raised the whip in the air,
The crowd cheered on my little grey mare.

Elsie Benneyworth (12)
St John's Marlborough, Marlborough

Hitman

My partner and I froze when we saw it
I grabbed my binoculars and saw him
The man was looking for us
We decided to move to the roof
There were many windows
We chose the front one
The laser cutter was immaculate
My partner chose the left
That left me with the other side
I heard footsteps
I found another hiding place
He walked and passed me
As I lined up my shot
I pulled the trigger...
I fainted!

Joe Bartlett (12)
St John's Marlborough, Marlborough

Alone

The guy you hurt in the corner of the room
died in a fire, he set the deadly fume

The one you called fat, she is sat over there
she is trying to forget but she can't be repaired

And the girl you pushed in the river
will now be teased about it forever

Why do you try and hide
what you are really feeling inside?

Everyone knows the reason you groan
it's because we all know you are alone.

Casey Berry (12)
St John's Marlborough, Marlborough

A New Home

Slam!
I'm shut in, tail between my legs,
My surroundings unfamiliar.
Click!
My paws pad on the cold floor of this warm place,
My surroundings unfamiliar.
Bang!
A creature nearly identical to me comes running to greet me,
My surroundings still unfamiliar.
Time passes.
I'm comfortable here now.
My surroundings are familiar,
Here is my new home.

Lauren Frost (13)
St John's Marlborough, Marlborough

Death

Lingering, I wait
In this world full of hate
Hiding in the shadows
I shall dispose

My heart is hollow
As I watch and follow
My soul is dark
As I leave my mark
I shall dispose

I have darkness inside
That I cannot hide
I have a burning urge
To complete a purge
I shall dispose

Just remember
I will never surrender
And I will always win.

Nancy Nicholls (13)
St John's Marlborough, Marlborough

Banana

I woke up this morning
I was still yawning
I am a banana but I taste like a sultana
I got shipped to Ghana
I'm in my box
But I see a lock
I feel like I'm in jail
Now I'm as slow as a snail

Now I'm in Ghana
Someone is going to eat a lovely banana
Ghana is nice
I see no mice
Ghana is dry
I look at the sky
Now I am dead
They ate my head!

Jontie Hart (11)
St John's Marlborough, Marlborough

Sam

I have a big brother called Sam
he likes to eat ham
he looks up to his dad called Dan
but he's still not much of a man

he looks like a frying pan
always applying fake tan
pulled up to school in a crusty white van
yet still thinks he's the man

he flies drones with a cam
whilst eating roast ham
and a sandwich filled with jam
now he's nearly a fat man!

Elsie Monro (13)
St John's Marlborough, Marlborough

Through The Eyes Of The Earth

Greta, Greta
you couldn't have done better
you've told the world
of what has evolved
you've saved the lives
of all that dies
thank you for what you have done.

People would say
you can't save the day
shut up and go away
you didn't give up
you showed them up
you did save the day
so don't fade away
thank you for what you have done.

Freddie Allen (13)
St John's Marlborough, Marlborough

Dogs

D ogs are fun to play with.
O bsessed with treats.
G ood at listening.
S oft like a teddy bear.

A mazing at catching sticks.
R eally loud when barking.
E xcited when meeting new people.

C uddles for ages.
U ltra friendly.
T errible at jumping.
E xcellent at making you feel better.

Tamzin Shipway (11)
St John's Marlborough, Marlborough

There Goes The Boat

T housands of people board the boat
I n ones and twos and threes and fours
T ime went on and problems occurred
A strange vibe was lingering
N ot knowing what was ahead, the ship carried on
I ce blocks appeared, getting bigger and bigger until
C *rash!* Cold, cold water surrounded the civilians as the Titanic met its final demise.

Issy Nuttall (13)
St John's Marlborough, Marlborough

Death And Life

I am Death
As lonely as anything
No one to love
No one to hug
I wish I could be like you
My duty is to bring great sadness
Why can't I bring life
Not kill it?

I am Life
I am as happy as anything
Everyone to love
Everyone to hug
I wish I could be like this forever
My duty is to bring joy
Why can't I stop Death?

Lewis Tearle (12)
St John's Marlborough, Marlborough

Left On A Page

I was suffocating
I couldn't breathe
But once I was found
My life started working

My blood is leaving
What's going to happen?
The sheets behead me
Are white no more
My life is going
Please help me

They told me I would be forgotten
My legs will need me no more
They will move on
And leave me as no one.

Lucy Josey (13)
St John's Marlborough, Marlborough

The Sadness Of War

Trapped in the unwelcoming darkness,
Only hearing echoes of sirens.
Knowing that death is upon me,
But there is nothing I can do.

Screaming and crying everywhere I go,
My heart gets flooded with sorrow.
Hoping this war will end soon,
As I just want to leave my room.

Bombs go off here and there,
The only thing I can do is glare.

Isabel Barnett (12)
St John's Marlborough, Marlborough

Donald Trump

D onald
O dd and crazy
N ever does anything about the world
A nnoying all the time
L oser, never a winner
D readful at doing his work

T rump is terrible
R ubbish at everything
U seless at his work
M ost of the time people hate him
P eople want him to leave.

Beatrice Harvard Taylor (11)
St John's Marlborough, Marlborough

Space

Another galaxy we pass,
My jets are roaring,
Travelling at light speed,
Through the midst of space.

My blue flames,
Leaving deadly black smoke,
Through the solid darkness,
That is space.

The way you see me,
I'm just a blur,
But I'm still there,
Travelling through the stars,
In space.

Max Potter (13)
St John's Marlborough, Marlborough

My Friend

I'm staring through the glass
As my owner takes out my friend
And wraps him in a cloth,
I don't know where he is going,
I go to where I slept
In the cove next to the pink rock
Then I go and stare out of the window
To where my owner has water on her face,
I am thinking,
Why am I called Grego the Third?

Alice Drowne (11)
St John's Marlborough, Marlborough

Coronavirus

The coronavirus has spread around countries
Originated from China
It came from the markets
So many animals have been hurt
Dogs, chickens and pigs
Skinned alive and left to die
Letting off the virus
Planes are being stopped
Some are still coming through
Could it really be serious
If you have got the flu?

Honey Lewis (12)
St John's Marlborough, Marlborough

A Fractured Mind

Rejection is a pain
Unparalleled by normal wounds
Cuts no matter how deep
Always heals
But will my scars?
Rejected by everyone around me
Standing alone
Despite the hundreds around me
Alone
Pushed away for being different
Despite those who try to help
I feel all alone
Separated
Rejected.

Thomas Norris (12)
St John's Marlborough, Marlborough

The Crow

I sit on a tree
I am lonely but free
I stare down at the children who play
Doing this day after day
How I wish I could be down there
Or just sitting on my chair
But instead I can fly
And soar through the sky
To a new place every day
To New York or LA
But I am just a crow
Who is free but alone.

Edie Liddiard (13)
St John's Marlborough, Marlborough

Bully

I bully others
Because you bully me

I loath you
And you loath me

I am forgotten and feared
Because of my family

My life is a miserable world
Thanks to you I hurl

You destroy me
Because I don't love you

I respect nobody
Because you don't respect me.

Lucy Morris (13)
St John's Marlborough, Marlborough

Time

I am the one stealing your age
Making you feel enraged
I am the one that lives forever
If you try to travel into the future
I will say never

I know I'm boring and sad
Which will make you mad
But you should thank me for you having a good life
You should thank me for your beautiful memories.

Stefan Pintilei (12)
St John's Marlborough, Marlborough

Death

See those fallen shadows?
Life slowly melting into death.
Those last days were not enough -
As souls we are descending into Hell.

Life devoured by those ghastly thoughts,
As you lay there; corpse-like, pasty-white.
Plunged into eternal sleep -
The dark place was waiting to capture you whole...

Megan Greenhalgh (13)
St John's Marlborough, Marlborough

Through The Eyes Of A Vegan

Healthy salad heaped upon my dish
Completely different from my ordinary fish
Green as envy, green as grass
I'm starting to wonder how long January will last
Oh how I long for some real food
I'm not really in the 'vegan' mood
Tender carrot, emerald pea
All of this, just to be healthy!

Una Lenehan (12)
St John's Marlborough, Marlborough

Time's Up

There's a child in bed,
Swirls of sorrow in her cup.
Monsters in her head.
I glance at the clock, time is up.
Gasp of this world's air,
Close her eyes, move aside her hair.
Azure paradise is near,
Although her essence I'm sucking,
Like every time, I feel nothing.

Lisa Nordlund (14)
St John's Marlborough, Marlborough

Jackie Chan Is An Amazing Actor

J ackie Chan is an amazing actor
A crobatics
C ool actor
K arate and martial arts
I nspiring many people
E nding for his acting? Never!

C alm
H and combat
A ttribute is kindness
N ever a bad actor.

William Mundy (11)
St John's Marlborough, Marlborough

Life

Uhhh, another day in the heat,
Wandering endlessly,
In the search for something I cannot find,
It will be like this till I lose my mind.
The savannah will never be forgiving,
Nor will the predators,
I just hope you don't take my little baby elephant!

Oscar Atkinson (13)
St John's Marlborough, Marlborough

Skeleton

Skeletons march around the street
Ready to steal all the children's sweets
Their bones rattle
Like a herd of cattle
I place sweets by the door
Only just past the town's store
Then I scream for my mum
And I start to suck my thumb!

Felix Sancto (12)
St John's Marlborough, Marlborough

Every Day

Every day he comes to visit me
His warm cheeks compacting my padding
His folds engulfing me
The curvature to his derriere
I am addicted to the scent of his hair wax
I feel so gifted
Then he leaves
And I am just
A chair
Again.

Theo Turner (12)
St John's Marlborough, Marlborough

Puppy Of The Game

S paniels surrounding the game,
P laying, playing,
A s cuddly as a polar bear,
N ever running out,
I love you and I hope,
E legantly fetching,
L eaping and diving,
S urrounded by toys.

Lois Stevens (12)
St John's Marlborough, Marlborough

Grandfather Clock

Ticking away
Through night and day
You bought me in the middle of May
You have to wind me every now and then
I usually stop at ten past ten
I bong every hour
And I am as tall as a tower
I go tick-tock
I am a grandfather clock.

Dakota Bessent (11)
St John's Marlborough, Marlborough

Death

Dark as the night, yet light as a feather
My heavy heart will drown you forever
No knife or gun, no weapon in sight
Yet I can kill you day and night
I end your pains to set you free
Your end's a beginning but there's no guarantee...

Elina Pfeiler (13)
St John's Marlborough, Marlborough

Tabby Cat

I am a curious cat
My brown tail swishes
I chase mice all day
I bring them inside
I sleep most of the day
And eat as well

I love my owners
Even if they are annoying
I love my food
But not my water
I am home.

Alice Seddon (12)
St John's Marlborough, Marlborough

The President

I am going to build a wall
It will be good and strong
And steady and tall
To keep out all the wrong
I am going to then get a new wig
Not flimsy and blond
I'll also get a new skin colour
But I'll never correspond.

Ted Rosedale (13)
St John's Marlborough, Marlborough

Freedom

The cold wind blew wildly, chilling their bones,
The trains blew their whistles, as they came to a stop.
The men in uniform yelled at the adults and children,
"Move along now. To the showers or to the huts."
One by one they went towards the showers or to the huts.

Families were separated, kids cried and adults pleaded,
But the choice was final and they were split up, separated,
From their loved ones to face the world by themselves.
Many faced trials and others death and labour.

The Nazi turned the showers on, but no water came.
Instead poisonous gas filled the room, killing everyone.
Their screams and cries went unheard, their bodies burned.

Thunder boomed and lightning flashed on this cold winter night.
Through their eyes they saw pain and suffering,
They watched families get split up and screams of pain,
Memories of sadness and sorrow, memories they'd never forget.

Through their eyes they saw freedom as the gates opened for them,
Soldiers came to take them away, to a place safe and sound.
Rescued safely they sipped warm cocoa and ate cookies.
They were finally free from that dreaded camp.

Zoe Webb (12)
The FitzWimarc School, Rayleigh

The Importance Of Education For Us All

For some, education and the consistency of the
School routine is the only constant in one's life; the only
Safe space for imaginations to soar freely,
For encouragement,
For gaining a sense of belonging.

For one to relinquish and deliberately surrender this
Opportunity defeats the object of the war fought to liberate
Students and galvanise minds into action and change for
the better.

For something Third World countries consider a rarity,
We take little regard of the importance it bears.
Malala Yousafzai campaigned so tirelessly for girls' rights
To education - even to the point she endured a gunshot wound
For representing her views.

Now, it seems her endeavours are not being acknowledged
And students take what some consider to be the root
Of success and prosperity for granted.

In the words of Malala, "One child, one teacher, one book, one
Pen can change the world."

Knowledge is power.

Ben Harris (15)
The FitzWimarc School, Rayleigh

Eye Of A Tiger

I live in a zoo,
And this is my home.
Full of life,
I'm the king of the throne.
Although I'm the ruler of my land,
I can't help feeling bored and sad.
So frustrated I feel inside this cage,
What I would do to release this rage.
I watch them shouting,
I watch them screaming,
Their faces always beaming.
They're scared of me,
But I don't know why,
All I feel is empty inside.
They watch me eat,
They watch me roar.
But all they want is more and more.
Days have passed but it's still the same,
Maybe one day things will change.

Mia Warwick (12)
The FitzWimarc School, Rayleigh

I Am Human

I am human, I can be brave
Strong to the grave,

Forever loving and bold
Whether young or old,

If I die I am remembered
Like a great fire to embers,

I lose time but it is of the essence
For all moons have a crescent,

I am human, forever brave
Accepting we are all going to the grave.

William Burling
The FitzWimarc School, Rayleigh

YOUNG WRITERS INFORMATION

We hope you have enjoyed reading this book – and that you will continue to in the coming years.

If you're a young writer who enjoys reading and creative writing, or the parent of an enthusiastic poet or story writer, do visit our website **www.youngwriters.co.uk**. Here you will find free competitions, workshops and games, as well as recommended reads, a poetry glossary and our blog. There's lots to keep budding writers motivated to write!

If you would like to order further copies of this book, or any of our other titles, then please give us a call or order via your online account.

Young Writers
Remus House
Coltsfoot Drive
Peterborough
PE2 9BF
(01733) 890066
info@youngwriters.co.uk

Join in the conversation!
Tips, news, giveaways and much more!

YoungWritersUK   **@YoungWritersCW**